COME WALK WITH ME

Healing Personal and Ancestral Grief

BY

Barbara J. Eatherly, M.Ed.

Dedication

For Big Dad and Big Mama,

who were both my parents and my grandparents.

Your agreement to be here now – and then –

made the healing opportunities in this book possible.

I love you throughout eternity.

Big Mama, Big Dad and Otelia
March, 1920

"There is only LOVE
and that that does not yet know itself as LOVE."
Lucy G. Destin, M.S, L.P.C. Lightworker,
Teacher and Friend

This book is the story of my soul's reincarnation into the same family to help heal the grief and sorrow created by my early passing in my last past life.

**Otelia on Easter
Sunday, 1921**

**Barbara on Easter
Sunday, 1951**

Acknowledgements

This book would not have been possible without the encouragement and support of many friends and colleagues.

First and foremost, I wish to thank my editor extraordinaire, Caroline Cottom, PhD. As poet, author, and editor, Caroline created a coherent manuscript from my notes and writings. The book would not have happened without her guidance and expertise. I am so blessed to have her in my life.

Many others provided expertise by reading and giving feedback on numerous drafts, including Diana Sullivan, Elizabeth Word, Patti Ingram, and Ruth Williams. My friend, Sydney McCain, a writer and educator, offered suggestions and ideas along the way to make my writing the best it could be. A special thanks also goes to Reverend Denise Yeargin and Jill Speering, who assisted me in letting go of the fear that prevented me from telling my story, as well as to those who shared their personal stories that are recounted in several chapters. Christian Sundberg's *A Walk in the Physical* helped me realize my connection to Otelia, which provided the framework for pulling my story together. The Shared Crossing Project, the work of Dr. William Peters, convinced me that many people have experiences similar to mine, thus helping me see that my story could have a life in mainstream culture. Lynadawn Farkas, lead researcher for the Shared Crossing Project, played a major role in encouraging me to move this project forward.

It is with great adoration and friendship that I also acknowledge Rick Weaver for his brilliant technical skills and friendship over the many years I have aspired to tell my story. Although we can go years without connecting, he always answers when I send out the call.

Finally, I am deeply indebted to those across the Veil who showed up to provide comfort, forgiveness, and love to me and so many others. I have been greatly blessed.

*****

Table of Contents

1

Seeking Answers

"Love is the bridge between you and everything." Rumi

My father was diagnosed with a rare blood disease when I was seven, which worsened throughout my adolescence until his death at the age of forty-six. I was nineteen years old when he died. Because I lacked any understanding of what was happening to him or why, I felt numb and worthless. In the midst of this, a special neighbor and my best friend's father died of cancer when I was thirteen. Unable to stop the inevitable, I became deeply depressed. The only way to function in my world was to act like people I cared about were not dying and that everything was fine.

What I lacked was a way to be with my father and my friend's father without feeling guilty about my inability to make them better. Like many people growing up in the 1950s and 60s, I had received no guidance. All the Bible School, Bible study lessons, and sermons I had been exposed to had not shown me how to be with someone who was dying. In those days, courses were not available in school or at church. It was a hush-hush subject. Denial was the way for most of us to handle our feelings.

This is still true today for many people, of course, but there are resources – books and videos – to assist us in facing death. The first book I read, ten years after my father's death, was *On Death and Dying* by Elizabeth Kübler-Ross, which describes five stages of grief: denial, anger, bargaining, depression, and acceptance. None of my family or friends had mentioned that there were stages of grief and perhaps had not even heard of them. In *On Death and Dying*, Kübler-Ross describes the stages from the perspective of the one who is dying, later coming to realize that loved ones go through similar feelings. Her later books speak directly to people like me, who grieved watching those I love die. When I read the description of grief and its stages, I immediately identified with every stage. I found great solace in realizing that what I had gone through was common and that many others had experienced the same denial and anger I felt after my father died.

Many books have been written sharing near-death experiences that offer reassurance concerning what a soul may encounter when one leaves the body. In *Dying to Be Me,* Anita Moorjani relates an experience she had while dying from fourth-stage cancer. Her body had shut down, and the doctors told her family that she had little time left. She recalls leaving her body, experiencing the peacefulness of "the other side," as well as the conversations and thoughts of those around her who were still on the Earth plane. She describes seeing her brother while he was on an intercontinental flight on his way to see her, hoping to get to her before she passed.

During her near-death experience, Moorjani met her father, with whom she had not had a strong connection while he was alive. He declared his love for her and his regret that he had not been present for her more often. This convinced her to return so she could clear up some of her own regrets before passing. Author and teacher Wayne Dyer heard her story and encouraged her to write a book about her experience. Moorjani's book and teachings have helped many people be less afraid of death.

Similarly, neurosurgeon Eben Alexander III, M.D., writes in *Proof of Heaven* how leaving his body changed his beliefs about death. While in a deep coma for seven days, his consciousness left his body to explore the afterlife. He relates that he went through a place of darkness before entering a place of peace and joy unlike anything he had experienced before. Prior to this experience, Alexander had not believed that prayer or anything else outside of science was capable of healing. His out-of-body experience allowed him to face his lifelong fear of death and expand his awareness of the possibilities of an afterlife. It also helped him to become more compassionate with his patients.

These books and others like them have helped many deal with their fear of death, but little has been written that provides assurance for the one who is close to death's door. Watching my aunts and uncles struggle with their feelings about dying as they neared the end of their lives, I wanted to do something – anything – that might help them. From this state of worry and grieving for them, I discovered a way I could assist.

My experiences offering solace to family and friends who were nearing death led me to write *Come Walk with Me*. In its pages are numerous examples of comforting others who are facing death, helping to alleviate their fear and angst about dying without having to go through a near-death experience.

As well, many in the Western world carry a fear of the punishment they will receive when they die, which many churches and families teach their children. My family and the church I grew up in taught me that I am a sinner and, no matter how I struggle to live up to God's expectation of perfection, I can never achieve the perfection of His Son, Jesus. In other words, "God will get you for that in the hereafter!" Who wouldn't fear death with that idea about their future?

This played out in my world through the baptism ritual at my church. We were expected to surrender our lives to Jesus Christ, who in turn would save us from our sins. I bought this hook, line, and sinker. When I was twelve years old, I "surrendered" and was baptized in front of the congregation. Three years later I surrendered again, because in my mind I had sinned beyond redemption and would never go to heaven. I don't know what I thought I had done that was so sinful between the ages of twelve and fourteen. Maybe it was kissing.

When I was eighteen, during the church service where "God will get you" was once again the theme, I walked out and down the street to my boyfriend's house and had a beer with him. I figured if I was going to hell anyway, I was going to have a heck of a good time getting there. I have learned since that God is love and has no desire to punish any of His children.

Fast forward to the passing of my grandmothers many years after my father's death. Dreams of the times spent in the rocking chair with my maternal grandmother, Big Mama, as well as learning to sew with my father's mother, sustained me during their illnesses and time of passing. However, not until I developed a meditation practice in order to *be* with them during those times did I become aware of just how powerful and comforting it was to sit in silence and see myself connecting with them, heart to heart, soul to soul. I've been amazed and pleased to discover that, similar to what happens in prayer, the recipient of my wishes for connection and love receives them. Connecting on a soul level has been supportive both to me and to my loved ones in transition, by replacing concern with a deep heart connection.

The stories in this book include examples of how connecting with our ancestors and others who have passed over can also give *us* a sense of peace and tranquility about what is to come. I call these experiences "walks" because they are simply visits to the other side of the veil. As well as assisting our loved ones in transitioning to the afterlife, one can also use the process I describe to assist people in search of emotional and spiritual healing. In my experience and the experiences of those who have utilized this process, the walks have spiritually and emotionally healed loved ones, relationships, and ourselves.

In video interviews and written materials, cardiologist Zach Bush, M.D., describes his work to bring back terminally ill patients whose hearts have stopped. Dr. Bush tells of the day he brought back three individuals in succession after they had died briefly in the ICU. The question each of them asked upon return was, "Why did you bring me back?" His patients reported experiences of unconditional love and acceptance greater than they could have imagined, and that they no longer feared death.

Dr. Bush came to understand that death is not a scary thing with devils taking you to eternal damnation, nor is it a place of nothingness. Rather, it is a place of deep acceptance and love. He suggests that we each need to have a "pre-death experience" to understand what it means to be a soul in a body; when the body dies, the soul lives on. In truth, my intention with *Come Walk with Me* is exactly that, to provide you and your loved ones with a pre-death experience.

Two books that have given me the most clarity are *A Walk in the Physical* by Christian Sundberg and *Testimony of Light* by Helen Greaves. Their words touched a knowing deep inside me and helped me understand that there is always more to learn. In the words of Sundberg, "Our primary reason for being here is the growth of 'what we are' toward love. What survives bodily death then is our true self – our "Beingness" –which retains its true nature. That is retained forever."

Over the years I have continued to explore the possibilities of what might await us after death of the body. The teachings of my childhood confused and traumatized me while I was experiencing the world around me and adjusting to the world within me. They just did not match my personal experience.

As a child it never occurred to me that leaving my body to "visit" loved ones or to travel to other locations was anything out of the ordinary. As far as I knew, everyone was doing the same thing. But

I learned very early not to talk about it. When I was nine years old, I shared one of my experiences with a close friend after Sunday School. A look of horror crossed her face.

"I'll pray for your soul!" Her eyes widened and her voice shook as if I had introduced her to the devil him or herself.

After this experience I kept my mouth shut. I only began to share my memories with others as I started to write about the visions I experienced on these walks. In addition to the personal healing mentioned above, the walks have opened me to more awareness of my early years and especially my relationships with my mother's family.

It is my wish and prayer that they will bring healing, comfort, and new awareness to you, too.

2

Welcome to My Journey

"Though this body has a beginning and an end,
the dweller in the body is infinite and without end."
Lord Krishna, The Vedas

Descending from the second floor at my grandparents' home, twelve wooden steps led to the four-foot by eight-foot landing, and another eight steps to the main floor. The steps were black, bounded by a black handrail that curved and was held up by white spindles. Once shiny, by the time I visited the house as a child, they were worn from years of feet treading up and down.

I was on my third or fourth trip bouncing down the stairs when I heard, "Mama, where are you?" A desperate voice.

My grandmother, Big Mama, appeared in the parlor, wiping her hands on her apron.

"Yes, dear, what do you need?"

"Don't you have something to keep this child out of here?" It was Big Dad, gruff, impatient.

I loved to spend time in their home as a child. My favorite place to play was on the stairs next to Big Dad's chair. I loved running up and down, bumping down on my bottom, and playing with my dolls on the landing. I often sang to the dolls while staging a party or practicing my favorite song of the day like "This Little Light of Mine." I loved demonstrating the hand gesture of hiding my light under a bushel and yelling "No!" as loud as possible. Playing Sunday school was another favorite pastime. The stories of Moses parting the seas and twelve-year-old Jesus speaking with the elders in the temple impressed me with their courage and boldness. I told those stories to my dolls a lot and embellished them more each time.

I could tell when Big Dad had had enough, because he would clear his throat loudly and huff through his nose, often snapping the newspaper. I know now that my constant movement and noise got on his nerves, big time. When he called Big Mama, he was usually at the end of his patience. It frightened me when he hit his wall of "enough is enough."

Big Dad was my mother's father. Stocky and 5'10'', he was bald with a horseshoe of white hair around the back of his head. He wore a white dress shirt with his hearing aid tucked in the front pocket and dress pants held up with suspenders, always ready to present himself as the owner of Lebanon, Tennessee's, small family funeral home. He seemed stiff to me and unapproachable, and I was careful not to get in his way. Even as a teenager I was cautious in his presence. Years later I remembered times that I had avoided him altogether.

Big Dad passed away when I was fifteen. I was sad for my mom and Big Mama, but I don't recall grieving his death. Big Mama lived for twenty-five more years, and I know she missed him, but once the funeral was over, I never thought much about him. Decades later I still felt distant, even in my memories of him.

I have often questioned why I've chosen to be single for thirty years, after two painful divorces. I had a lifelong fear of rejection that I'd held onto since I was a child, but I wasn't sure why. Feelings about my relationship with my grandfather would surface and gnaw at me, but I didn't understand the connection to my staying single. Finally, I sought out hypnotherapy, hoping it might help me let go of what was keeping me from having a successful primary relationship. Little did I know that the session would take me back to early impressions of my grandfather.

As I closed my eyes and listened to the hypnotist's voice, an image came of a dome of light where my grandfather and I were surrounded by people I knew to be our ancestors, although I was unable to distinguish who was who. Front and center stood Big Dad, who greeted me with a broad smile. He was younger than I remembered and had the hair of his younger years, which I had seen in photos—thick, dark brown hair, almost black, much like my mother's and mine had been before they started to turn gray. Dressed in a dark gray suit, similar to what he had worn to church, my grandfather looked extremely handsome to me.

"It is so good to see you again," he said. "You've grown up to look so much like your mother. Beauty still runs in the family."

This caught me by surprise. My memories did not include loving greetings or the warmth I felt from this smile. Standing in his presence took me back to the timid four-year-old, fearful that I would upset him.

Shaken, I said, "I don't understand why you were always so gruff and impatient with me.

I was afraid to get in your way. Please tell me why."

"I'm happy to have the chance to tell you what was going on when you were young." His eyes shone as he spoke. "Talking didn't come easy for me. Now you know about Otelia, the daughter we lost when she was almost four years old, shortly before your mother was born."

"What does that have to do with me and the way you reacted to me?"

"In the early years, when you would visit us, you reminded me so much of Otelia. I couldn't separate the two of you in my heart." He placed his right hand over his heart. "I am so sorry I frightened you. I never meant to hurt you. I just couldn't tolerate the pain I was feeling. Your laugh and giggle sounded as if Otelia were right there! Please forgive me. I love you, and I always have."

I could feel the tenderness and kindness in his voice.

Then I became aware of Big Mama standing beside him. With an understanding smile, she laid her head on his shoulder, a loving gesture I had seen many times before.

He affectionately turned to her with a sigh. "I am at peace, my dear."

The image faded into a white glow, and I became aware of the room where I was sitting. I felt a rush of love for my grandfather. The confusion, fear, and anger I'd held onto from those early years were gone. Tears filled my eyes.

It is difficult to put into words the profound relief I felt after encountering my grandfather in this way. Some might say that it was my imagination, but the change I felt was palpable, and the healing of my feelings about him was as real as if I had spoken to him in person. After this session, I sat thinking about the many times I had felt fear and confusion when I was with him.

Those feelings had just been altered to encompass the love he had actually felt for me.

The hypnotherapy session followed many years of connecting with other family members, with friends, and even with animals, on what I have come to call "walks." I did this while sitting in silent meditation and asking to connect with them, heart to heart. The walks took place over many years and did not follow a particular timeline.

My earliest memory of my consciousness leaving where I was physically to go be with someone somewhere else is when I was three years old. When I was put down for a nap and wanted to be with my dad on his afternoon off, I would visit him in his workshop, a place I wasn't allowed to go because of the dangerous tools and objects that "could hurt little girls." I would see my dad in the workshop sanding a piece of wood and imagine myself going through the forbidden doorway to watch him more closely.

I have continued to "walk" throughout my life, especially when I missed someone I loved or had a misunderstanding and wanted to clear it up immediately. Most walks involved meeting with family members who were no longer in their physical bodies. On some of the walks, I reunited with friends and other loved ones who had crossed over after death, or there was unfinished business they and I needed to complete. Others were with my pets or those belonging to a friend. Many of the people and animals in my stories have now passed on; others knew they were dying and were frightened because they did not know what to expect. Several other people have more recently initiated walks with their loved ones after learning how to use this process.

I have come to understand how the grief we carry based on losses and misunderstandings affects our relationships. In all cases, my purpose in taking the walks was to assist others – and myself – in healing our relationships. I have kept journals of the walks, which I share now in the spirit of supporting others on their path to creating more loving and compassionate relationships and to healing anything that is unlike love.

Come Walk with Me includes my perceptions of how my walks have affected my family, mostly my mother's family of origin. Some of the memories are from third-party perceptions that I relate here in my own words and include my interpretation of what took place. In no way are they intended to speak for others, as each person has his or her own memories and interpretations. The most important aspect of the interactions with others has been honest communication and loving expression about particular events to provide clarity and understanding.

My hope is that this book will open others to the possibilities that are available to us when we clear away our judgments and limited ideas about our loved ones. As well, most of us carry beliefs about what awaits us after death that are based in fear – beliefs about endings and loss. The walks carried assurances that death is not the end. I believe this to be true. In the words of the Vietnamese monk Thich Nhat Hanh, death is "only a change of clothes."

So much more is available to us if we open ourselves to living from a place of allowance, acceptance, and love. Taking walks for the purpose of healing painful relationships and gaining clarity, in my experience, is one powerful way to accomplish this.

Perhaps you will want to try this process yourself. Indeed, it is my hope that you do. If so, I've included a brief description of how to do it as a part of the book.

3

Not a Galaxy Far, Far Away

"There is no try, you either do or do not." Yoda

Our family moved into a new home the summer I turned six years old, a home that would be big enough for my parents, my three brothers, and me. My father and older brother Wayne had worked on the house during the spring and most of the summer to get it ready. Contractors built the frame, and Wayne and Dad did the finishing work and the roof. Hard work! There were four bedrooms: one for me, the only girl; one for Wayne, the oldest. John and Jake shared the largest room, and Mom and Dad would finally have some privacy. Before the move, my parents' bedroom was in the center of the house, and we kids ran through it like it was a hallway. It's amazing, thinking back on it, that they didn't seem to mind.

Included were two acres of pasture and an old cattle barn. Dad made a workshop out of the front part of the barn, and the back eventually became home for a variety of animals. We had a pony once, and Dad had also tried to raise chickens. That's another book in itself! The yard was ours for playing badminton, horseshoes, basketball, ping pong, even softball and football.

Behind our property was a large field with a pond for watering the cattle. Dad also built a playhouse, and the boys built a fort in the back of the pasture. My parents hoped that the kids in the neighborhood would hang out in our yard so they would know where we were, and it worked. We spent many hours climbing in the large maple tree next to the cattle pond.

In the new house, I finally had a girlfriend to play with, one who lived right across the street and even shared my birthday. With three brothers, plenty of boys came around, but very few girls who would brave our yard. Ann and I became great friends, spending time in both of our houses and yards. We loved to play on a bar swing her father had built in their back yard. Chains that were ten feet long hung from another bar anchored into a tree and a pole. We would play trapeze performers by hanging by our knees, and when we were really brave, by our ankles.

Ann had an older sister and was used to girl things; with my three brothers, I was familiar with boy stuff. She had an abundance of dolls and a trunk full of clothes for dress-up. When her sister outgrew something or went to a fancy dance, we dressed up and pretended we went, too.

At my house, by contrast, there was every kind of ball imaginable, great trees to climb, and the pond we loved to sneak off to and explore.

During my family's first year in that house, Ann's mother created a large playroom upstairs for Ann and her toys. It was the best room ever. Dolls were everywhere. Ann's mom was a great seamstress and used the scraps leftover from dance dresses, fur jackets, and even swimsuits to make doll clothes and play clothes for us. There were stacks of games like Candy Land, Monopoly, and cards for Go Fish or Slap Jack. I loved to spend time in that playroom.

Ann and I were very competitive. What one did, the other had to do better. Let's just say we were both stubborn. At one point, our moms insisted we take a break from each other. One night after our moms had separated us for arguing, I lay in my bed thinking of how much I missed Ann's toys and how much I really, really, really wanted to go play with them. While picturing the room in detail, I invented the game of "fly over." I focused on the window in my room, then I pictured the top of the cherry tree outside my window. From the cherry tree I could see the window at the end of their house where I could peek inside the playroom and enter the playroom. Wow! I was actually there! It was very real to me. I imagined playing for a long time before my awareness returned to my bed.

After "flying over" several nights, I got tired of playing alone so I pictured myself by Ann's bed and got her to come play with me. It was so easy. While we were playing, we got loud enough in the ethers to wake her mother. All of a sudden, I heard, "Whoever is up there making that noise, you better leave *now* and never come back!"

Immediately I was in my bed, afraid of provoking her mother's ire. That was the last of my nighttime "flyover game" and out-of-body adventures until many years later.

Fast forward to when I was separated from my eight-year-old son during divorce proceedings. I was in deep pain not being with him every day, especially at bedtime. A counselor suggested I connect with him in my mind and heart and send him my love before I went to sleep at night. That's when I recalled visiting the playroom doing the flyover.

One night I decided to breathe deeply and mentally connect through my heart to his heart. I visualized Ray on his Star Wars sheets, with the Star Wars curtains next to his navy-blue desk where the Millennium Falcon was parked, ready to take off. After a few more breaths I found myself looking at my child sound asleep. The first time I just sent loving thoughts and hugs to him. When I found myself back in my own bed, I was crying with joy and felt more peaceful than I had since the drama around the divorce began.

As I continued my nighttime visits, Ray would chat about his day. He was fond of the book, *Planes, Trains and Automobiles*, which had a hidden Gold Bug throughout the book for little minds to find. He always remembered where the Gold Bug was on each page; I always forgot. He would giggle at me. Often, we would laugh about something silly he had experienced that day. Ray was already interested in music and liked playing the guitar. Sometimes he would show me something he had learned, excited to get out of bed to pick up the guitar.

Of course, I never left my home. These visits sustained me in my grief over many months and extended into years. Even though Ray is in his forties now and a father himself, I still make a visit to check on him from time to time. I've recently started to visit my granddaughter as well.

We'll see where that goes.

Through these experiences with my son, I learned how to connect with loved ones in my heart and mind for the purpose of healing, forgiveness, and sharing love with them. Meditating and "visiting" my son promoted a deeper connection and helped me heal wounds over the loss I was carrying due to the divorce. Being able to feel him over a long distance also enabled me to be more authentic when we were together face to face.

Since early childhood I had stuffed my feelings in the name of survival or fitting in. Only now am I beginning to realize the importance of allowing all my feelings to be okay. I often have "distance" conversations with my son on issues like disciplining his daughter. In my meditation I can say exactly what I want without fear of repercussions or outrage from my son. Of course, I would do it differently if we were actually together. Wouldn't it be grand if we could be that honest in person!

4

Fix It or Deny It

*"Open your heart and you will open your eyes
to a new way of seeing." Suzanne Giesemann*

My job has always been to fix things, make things better, even at the expense of my own happiness. I cannot tolerate those I love to be in pain, sorrow, or even just unhappy. When someone I care about is in pain for any reason, I feel a need to fix it, and if I can't find a way to do that, I deny it. That is how I have dealt with many of my relationships over the years, but the relationship that suffered the most was my relationship with my dad during the years of living with his blood disorder, from the time I was seven until I was nineteen. Because I was powerless to heal him, I resorted to denial.

As the disease progressed, our family, which was otherwise loving and supportive, became fragmented. Each of us tended to focus on our own lives—school, sports, church, and social activities with friends. From the beginning, the doctors were perplexed about what was causing my dad's body to destroy his white blood cells. They had ruled out leukemia and explored other options without success. As a child, I dropped in on adult conversations, feeling lonely and afraid, not knowing what was going on. Of course, the adults never thought to include a seven-year-old in their discussions.

My dad worked as manager of Sears and Roebuck in Murfreesboro, Tennessee, and did woodworking and refinished furniture in his spare time. One afternoon our family doctor, Dr.

Shacklett, came to the house to go through Dad's workshop in the old barn. I tagged along. As he examined the paints and refinishing agents to determine if one might be the culprit, I heard words that were unfamiliar and scary. I had been warned in the past to stay out of the barn and away from the chemicals, so I knew they were dangerous. The best I could figure out was that no conclusion resulted from the visit. The adults were still in the dark as to what caused my father's illness.

Without a diagnosis, there could be no cure. Doctors used what treatments they had available at the time to keep my father alive as long as possible, not knowing how long that would be. Over the next twelve years, Dad was in and out of the hospital and put on steroid medications that changed his personality. He was more irritable and drank often during my high school years. At one point he broke his leg falling out of a boat and was in a cast up to his groin for four months. Despite the pain and confusion caused by the medications, my father continued to go to his job, until it became obvious that the treatments were no longer keeping him stable.

During my freshman year in college, I acted out my family's turmoil and despair around his dying. Like many teenagers, I was extremely self-centered, focusing on destructive love affairs and rowdy behaviors. I drank and spent time with drinkers and partiers. I had a boyfriend my dad didn't like at all. My mother told me, "If you don't stop misbehaving, you're going to kill your father."

As my father's disease worsened, I left home for that same boy, moved into a rented room, got a job at the State Farm regional office filing papers eight hours a day, and dropped out of college.

During my brief departure into the world of filing cabinets and insurance policies, I was able to mend my relationship with Dad. He had quit drinking and was attending Alcoholics Anonymous meetings, which opened the door for more sincere conversations. I approached him about my moving back home and returning to school. He and Mom had paid my freshman year tuition and books while I lived at home, so Dad's response shocked me. "How do you propose to pay for college now?"

He made me a deal that if I paid the tuition for the fall semester I could move back home, provided I helped my mom and stopped running with the party crowd. My last paycheck from the insurance company was $93.10, and tuition for the semester was $94.30. Mom slipped me the $1.20 difference.

During those years Dad entered the hospital often and slept a great deal. The disease required many blood transfusions, and doctors later assumed some of the blood was tainted with hepatitis and HIV/Aids. He contracted serum hepatitis during the last few months of his life, which doctors believe shortened his life considerably.

In September 1967, just after I moved back home, Dad entered the hospital for the last time. While he was in the hospital and near death, I visited him only once. I cringed when I saw him. It was not my dad in that bed. He was retaining fluid because of the hepatitis and was so swollen that he was unrecognizable.

While Mom traveled 35 miles back and forth to the hospital in Nashville from Murfreesboro to hold vigil for him, I went about my life as if nothing was wrong. It didn't matter that my family and the doctors were telling me my father would not live much longer. I refused to go back to see him, acting like everything would return to normal. My father had been in the hospital many times over the past twelve years, so I convinced myself he would come home again.

He died in January, unable to come home for the holidays or for his 46th birthday that December. The night he passed away, I knew it even before Mom entered the house. I had heard the car pull in the driveway and met her at the back door. I could tell by the look on her face and the energy surrounding her that his suffering was over. She was spent and could give nothing more.

Although I didn't talk to my father those last few weeks, I remember feeling love between us, then and in times before. Every time I thought of him while he was dying, after he went to the hospital the last time, I cried, praying he would come home.

How I managed to return to school and complete my degree was definitely a "God thing." I wasn't conscious of any of the choices I was making. While finishing school I worked three jobs: one in the Health, Physical Education and Recreation office at MTSU, another selling clothes for a boutique, and at night as a dental assistant for a dentist who was just starting his practice. If it hadn't been for needing the money and working so much, I probably would have continued on my self-destructive path.

Dad died in the winter of my sophomore year. For most of my junior and senior years, I blocked out the pain completely. I was so angered by my helplessness that I did not grieve the loss of my father until I was thirty-six years old. When my first marriage fell apart, that loss triggered the feelings I had suppressed during my father's illness and death. The end of my marriage was yet another death.

This new crisis catapulted me into finding answers to questions about dying, grief, and loss through therapy. My mother's words echoed in my mind, "If you don't stop acting this way, you are going to kill your father." When I finally began to grieve for my father, my mother's words haunted me. Guilt and shame rose up with a vengeance.

In time I was able to forgive myself for my behavior and the grief I had caused my mom and dad.

5

A Girl Like Me

*"With life as short as a half-taken breath,
don't plant anything but love." Rumi*

For most of my life I've believed that my caretaking and fix-it personality began to develop when I was seven upon learning my dad had a serious disease, but I recently discovered that my caretaking feelings go back to the summers when I visited my grandfather, Big Dad.

In the guided hypnotherapy session I described previously, an image came to me of my grandfather as I knew him when I was five years old. I became aware of how afraid I was of his gruffness and impatience with me. Later, as an adult, I had learned from family stories that he was a humanitarian, deeply caring of everyone he encountered and always helping others. He was elected to public office in his late fifties as a trustee for Wilson County, Tennessee, where he was assigned to handle unemployment benefits. I heard stories of how my grandparents fed drifters on their back porch during the Great Depression. Through these stories, I came to understand that he was, in fact, a generous, caring man, contrary to what I felt and believed as a child.

Each fall of my elementary years, before starting school, I would visit my mom's parents, Big Mama and Big Dad, in Lebanon, Tennessee. My grandparents lived in a southern colonial home with stout white columns and a wraparound porch, across the road from a private college.

On the porch were half a dozen Adirondack chairs and ferns in concrete urns, and over the entrance to the front door was a sign that read "Funeral Home." The sign was lit up whenever my grandparents opened their home for a visitation or a funeral.

Because my grandfather was an undertaker, their home also served as a funeral parlor when needed. Downstairs were two generous-sized rooms that had been converted into a viewing room and a chapel with a piano. Next to the viewing room was a large dining room with a table that my grandmother filled with homemade goodies whenever a visitation and funeral took place: southern fried chicken, potato salad, baked beans, and other dishes, many of which the community contributed.

At the back of the house was a country kitchen with its large enamel sink and well water pump left over from when there was no running water in the house and, attached to the kitchen, a mudroom for leaving our shoes when we came in from working in the garden. Next were my grandparents' bedroom and bathroom, and a secret room that was off limits to my cousins and me. As a young child I observed bodies coming and going from that room and would not learn until I was ten that it was where my grandfather embalmed the bodies.

Upstairs was a small apartment where Uncle Leon and Aunt Jan lived when they were first married, plus three more bedrooms and a bathroom. An extra wide hall opened onto other rooms that were large enough for a daybed. I slept on a cot in my grandparents' bedroom until I was old enough to sleep upstairs in the room that had been my mom's and that she had shared with her sister, Yvonne. Across the hall from that room was a smaller room where Big Dad's mother stayed during her final years, cared for by Big Mama. Granny "Down on the Pike," as they called her, hated her circumstances and yelled at Big Mama often, so my cousins and I avoided her and that room.

The summers I stayed in my mother's old room, I relished rummaging through drawers and closets to find anything I could about her. Sometimes I found treasures like letters from an old boyfriend I hadn't heard of, a letter sweater from high school, or pictures of people unfamiliar to me who I knew would have been important to her.

It was a treat to go to my grandparents' house to get one-on-one time away from my three brothers. I loved being with Big Mama. Big Dad, not so much. He would turn off his hearing aid when I was around because I was too loud and way too energetic for him.

At the bottom of the stairs was an alcove with a blond oak desk and chair and a large window where Big Dad read the newspaper, the Bible, and other papers that looked boring to me. He became angry when I bounced down the steps and would call Big Mama to come stop me and make me settle down. This was fine with me, as she would kindly march me to the kitchen to help with one of her many tasks. I loved being in the kitchen with her. We made sugar cookies and biscuits, and, when I was five years old, she taught me how to sew my first skirt: a gathered red print skirt made from flour sacks, with a waistband. That was the beginning of my love of sewing. I was very proud of that skirt and didn't want to take it off. I even wore it over my shorts when I played outdoors.

The week was not all fun and games, however. Behind the garage was an acre garden that my grandparents tended, and a shed for a plow horse and cow. Big Dad expected me to help with weeding and picking, but I would sneak off to the playground in the schoolyard behind the garden, slipping through a hole in the fence just big enough for me to squeeze through. When he spotted me on the swings instead of pulling weeds or picking beans, he would call me to come "this instant," as he couldn't get through the hole in the fence. I never wanted to obey, but I knew better than to defy him. Big Mama would take me off his hands to help her with something designed to distract me, like feeding the chickens. Needless to say, working in the garden was my least favorite part of my visit.

Big Mama had hair that hung to her waist, which she wore braided in a bun on the back of her neck. In the garden she and Big Dad both wore straw hats, weather-worn from the sun and stained with sweat. I'd seen photos of Big Mama when her hair was the color of ravens, but when I was a child, it was salt-and-pepper. She brushed it one hundred strokes each night. I often helped her brush her hair, and with patience she taught me to braid it.

On her dressing table was a picture of a small girl of about three years old. I thought it was a photo of me. The girl was standing on a sidewalk wearing a dress with a matching coat, MaryJane shoes, and an Easter bonnet decorated with flowers. She held a purse across her chest. The girl's hair was cut short around a sweet face and broad smile. I asked Big Mama where she got the photo, as I didn't remember having a dress like the one in the picture. Big Mama picked me up, put me on her lap, and told me it was Otelia, her first-born daughter, who had passed away when she was about my age. I sat in silence for what seemed like a long time.

Once Big Mama told me about Otelia, I wanted to know more. Big Mama had a wooden rocking chair in her bedroom that faced the window, where she sat in the mornings to read her Bible and pray. I loved to crawl into her lap when I first woke up, and now I began asking her to tell me more about Otelia. Although it seemed to make her sad, it seemed to also bring her joy. Her eyes would fill with tears, then she would give me a big smile. I think that smile is the reason I kept asking for more stories.

She told me how happy Otelia was, that she was always dancing around and singing. Her favorite song was "Jesus Loves Me," which was also the first song I learned to sing. Otelia had an imaginary playmate she called Barba. According to Big Mama, Otelia and Barba were together all the time. They played in the side yard under a huge weeping willow tree and danced around the tree, skipping and laughing. When Big Mama described it, I felt I was there.

Otelia died when Big Mama was pregnant with my mother. Barba had been so present in their lives that Big Mama and Big Dad named my mother Barba, which Mother changed to Barbara in high school.

Although I didn't connect the dots until much later, being in the rocking chair with Big Mama was my first knowing that I had been Otelia in a previous lifetime. Years later I would hear that Otelia had died of respiratory problems, another link I share with her.

Since fourth grade, I have had major attacks of bronchitis three or four times a year.

As I've shared, I realized I had been afraid of my grandfather. He was often gruff with me and never seemed happy to have me around. I didn't think he liked me, much less loved me, although this changed as I grew older. Our relationship became easier, I think now, because I was no longer the little girl who reminded him of Otelia.

My grandparents had five more children over the twelve years following Otelia's passing: my mother Barbara, Yvonne, Doris, Leon, and Everett. They all lived very different lives, but the theme of wanting to make their parents happy and proud was common to them all.

Many of my walks have involved those five children and how their lives were affected by the loss of the sibling they never knew. On my walks with them, each one played a part in the transformation of the grief and shame of the family. I first walked with my Uncle Everett, my mother's youngest brother and since then have walked with other family members to experience "the other side." Every time I have taken someone for a walk to check out what they can expect or might encounter when they transition out of their body, Otelia is present. This is true even when a walk is about reconciliation in a relationship outside my family. I have come to understand that Otelia, as the common thread among all my experiences, is my connection to the other side of the veil.

In the visions, Otelia is still the four-year-old girl who passed away from a bronchial infection on December 6, 1921. She appears in the front between her parents, my grandparents. She rarely speaks and always radiates light into the Dome of Light where the walks take place.

The fact that my grandmother was pregnant with my mother at the time of Otelia's passing was never talked about in the family. However, whenever Otelia was mentioned, Big

Mama would sigh and mumble something about "her baby." For me, it felt like a silent prayer of remembering and longing. Mother was born in May 1922, a little over six months after Otelia passed. Big Mama didn't have much time to grieve Otelia's loss as her days were consumed with home, church, and her new baby girl. Big Dad was selling cars at the time, trying to make his way in the world.

Ever since Big Mama began sharing stories about Otelia, I've known there is a strong connection between Otelia and myself. The photo of her in her Easter finest is almost identical to one of me at the same age. The two photos are framed together in my office as I write these words.

Before Otelia became ill, she played with her imaginary playmate, Barba. She loved to sing Bible songs, play Vacation Bible School, and entertain her dolls under the stairs – so similar to what I later did. Although she had changed the spelling to Barbara, my mother was always Barba to me. When I was born, my mother named me Barbara, also after Otelia's imaginary playmate. Otelia had not met any of her siblings on the Earth plane, so on the walks she is openly excited to connect with all of them. I believe she has been watching over them for a long time.

When the visions first began during my meditations, the first image was of Otelia, Big Mama, and Big Dad surrounded by ethereal images of other family members. We stood in what I can only describe as a dome of light. All those who were not participating in the "visit" were opaque with a glow that gave them form but no distinctive characteristics unless they came forward to participate in the dialogue. When this happened, they presented characteristics that I recognized. Otelia was always front and center, often jumping up and down with glee: a four-year-old who sees someone she loves.

NOTES

6

The Things We Never Say

*"Between what is said and not meant,
and what is meant and not said,
most of love is lost." Kahlil Gibran*

My first experience of taking a walk to the other side was with my uncle, Mom's youngest brother, Everett. He had stepped in after my father passed away and had become an important figure in my life. Whenever I needed to make a major decision, I went to him for advice. When I was debating whether to leave home and take a teaching job in South Carolina, Everett helped me explore my options, but he never told me what to do.

At seventy-six, Everett had the first of several mini strokes. A large man with a loving, commanding presence, he found it difficult to lose control, and his family was devastated watching him struggle with the after-effects of the strokes. It was difficult for me to witness his decline, too. My feelings of helplessness surged again.

To console myself, while doing my morning meditations and prayers, I began to speak to his heart from my heart. In those conversations I expressed love and gratitude for all he had done for me. I also asked forgiveness for those times I was disrespectful, such as the time I showed up for a family July 4th celebration a little tipsy, which was totally inappropriate for our family.

During these quiet times I saw him as young and vibrant, not in the compromised, declining state his body had taken on. When we would "meet," the energy was loving and peaceful, filled with a glow I can only describe as heavenly. I was meditating daily, and almost every day I had these visions of connecting with him on a heart level. As the months moved on, I continued the meditations and prayers, and visions began to appear of crossing with him to the other side to see what it might be like there. I was reading Eben Alexander's *Proof of Heaven*, and it occurred to me to ask Everett in meditation if he'd like to see what it is like once we die.

I assured Everett that I was not asking him to die, that he had a choice to stay or go back into his earth body. I told him that he was in charge of when his soul left his body, and no one could do it for him without his permission.

Evidently, he agreed because we were transported into a vast dome of translucent white light across from a large gathering of what I came to realize were our ancestors. Many were in the background and unrecognizable. However, front and center and very prominent were his mother and father (Big Mama and Big Dad), my father, and Otelia.

I also saw my grandfather's sister, Aunt Essie, in the brown mink fur shawl she always wore, winter and summer. I knew most of the relatives in the forefront; some I did not. Despite not knowing all of them, I was overwhelmed with the feeling of love that emanated from the assembled group, and somehow I knew they were all there in love.

My uncle and I stood about fifteen feet in front of the group. He and his mother, my grandmother, began to communicate telepathically. To my amazement, I could understand what they were saying.

Big Mama exclaimed, "I am so very proud of you. You have shown such love and gratitude for what we provided for you growing up, and you've passed on the legacy of our family courageously."

My grandmother seemed so joyful to be in his presence again. She shared how proud she was that he had lived his life with integrity. She expressed gratitude that he had taken such good care of her emotionally and financially after my grandfather passed on. Everett likewise expressed gratitude for the care with which they raised him to be a good Christian, as well as the family legacy of integrity and responsibility that had modeled for him how to watch over those in his care. They both seemed overwhelmed to reconnect and expressed love and joy at their reunion with warm smiles and words.

After a short time, Everett told me he was ready to return. I felt that he was testing me to see if he was really in charge. We smiled deeply at each other, and I immediately found myself back in my meditation chair, with tears of love and joy on my cheeks.

Over the next six months we took several walks to check out the other side. On our walks, Everett always chose to come back, as he had no desire to leave his wife, children, and grandchildren, even though he was failing physically more each day. The more we walked, the more he seemed to realize there was no separation between us and those we love, even after they or we have passed on. Only the physical separation that occurs at death gives us this perception. Everett demonstrated this to me several times on our walks by exploring more and more difficult conversations with his parents. He acted as if he were talking to them in the living room of his home. One of these talks included a discussion about how my grandfather had embarrassed Everett when he played football for the University of Kentucky.

My grandfather told him, "I know I stepped out of line many times when you were playing football, especially that time I decided to direct traffic so the team bus could get out of traffic."

Everett chuckled. "Well, the team got a kick out of 'that silly ole man in the middle of that traffic thinking he could move us out of there.' I was proud that you had the courage to direct traffic for a Kentucky bus in the middle of a Tennessee crowded parking lot when we had just defeated the home team!"

I could feel the air of pride from them both.

Otelia seemed delighted to finally meet her little brother. She laughed, "You are so big! I would love to ride on those big shoulders."

"It's great to meet you, little sis." He laughed as he bent down to her eye level. Even though the veil did not part enough for them to touch physically, I could feel that they were definitely connected. Had Otelia lived, she would have been Everett's eldest sister. I was amazed that Everett and Otelia knew each other immediately. I could feel the affection radiating between them.

On one of the walks, my dad told Everett, "It was painfully difficult to leave my wife and my family, although it was time for me to go. I am grateful to you for stepping up to help them over the years. We have been blessed by your generosity and love. I do not know what they would have done without you. Thank you. Love to you, my brother."

It seemed that all perceptions of separation dissolved as Everett and the ancestors stood in each other's presence.

On July 7, 2007, when I went to my meditation chair to send love and connect with Uncle Everett, I saw myself standing beside him in the nursing home, looking down at his emaciated body, where he was surrounded by his wife and children. When I asked if he wanted to walk with me, we were immediately in the familiar Dome of Light facing our ancestors. This time I noticed a new figure with a hound's tooth, short-brim fedora standing directly behind his mother and father that I had not noticed before. It was football coach, Bear Bryant! My uncle had played football for Bear Bryant in Kentucky, and they had remained close lifelong friends. During the walk, the respect and appreciation they had for each other was radiated in their smiles.

The most unusual thing about this walk was that Otelia ran to Everett with such joy and giggling with love that he reached down, picked her up, and placed her on his shoulders.

Immediately he was young and vibrant, as he had been in his early thirties. I was reminded of the many times in my youth he had lifted me the same way.

In all the visits that Everett and I had taken together, this was the first time there was physical contact. It was then I knew that he had decided to stay.

Suddenly, my meditation ended, and I was back in my chair. My eyes filled with tears as I rose to go make coffee. Walking down the hall, I began singing a favorite hymn of the family, "When the Roll Is Called Up Yonder." I had not thought of the hymn in years, much less sung it.

Thirty minutes later my cousin called to say that Everett, her father, had passed. I was humbled and felt blessed to have been present for that day's walk with my uncle.

At the memorial service, the song leader announced we would sing "When the Roll Is Called Up Yonder," which was also one of Everett's favorite hymns. While we sang, in my mind's eye I saw the ancestors all around the ceiling of the chapel, just as they had greeted us on our walks. Otelia was on his shoulders as he stood between his mother and father, with Bear Bryant in the recognizable fedora hat and the others nearby, celebrating the life of this great man.

All who had known and loved him were in agreement that he had been a generous and loving man throughout his life by supporting his family, his friends, and often strangers that showed up at his office needing to be acknowledged and guided to their next step.

The best way to describe the vision is to relate it to the ending scene in Star Wars when Luke sees Obi-wan Kenobi, Darth Vader, and Yoda in the Light.

I boohooed a lot.

7

In the Shadows

"Sometimes quiet people have a lot to say....
They just keep being careful
about who they open up to." *Susan Gale*

Over the next few years, my experiences with family illness and death increased, especially in my parents' generation, as all of them grew older.

Mother had a mild heart attack in 2004, which nudged me to take early retirement, sell my home in Hermitage, Tennessee, and move back to my hometown of Murfreesboro to live with her in her home. These events and others opened me to a new way of being in the world. Not working full-time gave me the opportunity to study different belief systems and forms of meditation. I studied Access Consciousness techniques and became a teacher of an energy healing modality called Transference Healing. At the same time, I was focused on mending whatever separation existed between my mother and myself. Taking care of an aging parent, what some might feel as a burden, I experienced as a powerful time of healing and reconnection.

In 2007, while I was living with my mother, her brother Leon, two years older than Everett, was diagnosed with heart disease. His health declined significantly over the next couple of years, and I decided to begin each day's prayer and meditation with Leon as the focus. These experiences were entirely different than the expansive experiences I had had with Everett. Even though I felt Leon's presence on the walks we took to check out the other side, I felt very little connection with him. I believe now that I was too concerned about the outcome and did not step out of the way enough for our hearts to come into alignment. I learned from this experience that humility is crucial to allowing the process to flow.

My fondest memories of Uncle Leon are about the way he told family stories. The most memorable was the "silent night" tale about my mother playing the piano and commanding her younger siblings to "act right." He always made us laugh, even though he told the same story over and over. He was also a master craftsman. Leon's work with wood earned him recognition not only in the family but in the woodworking community throughout the state of Kentucky. He and a friend built a grandfather clock from scratch, except for the clock mechanism, which was displayed in an artisan museum in Kentucky. He also played the banjo and to my recollection made one of his own. He had put himself through school and worked as a civil engineer for a gas pipeline company in Kentucky. There were sides to him I wish I had gotten to know better. We only got together for brief visits since he and his family lived outside Tennessee. The visits were typically holidays or other special occasions with many people around, which did not make for close, intimate conversations.

I thought that Uncle Leon had always felt like the stepchild in the family. Everett was a bright shining star, casting a long shadow on his older brother. Even as a child, I saw that my grandfather treated Leon differently, expecting him to be more like Everett. Big Dad didn't approve of the woman Leon married and felt that Leon was too softhearted, not man enough. He could cry on a dime. Every time he told a story, he would cry. To my grandfather, who was in the funeral business, you couldn't stand around and cry while hauling corpses out to the hearse.

When we first arrived in the Light and Otelia grinned at Leon, Big Dad said with a look of gratitude, "Let me look at you. It feels like I am really seeing you for the first time."

Big Dad paused to look at his son's face and then to take in Leon's physical stature. "I was always consumed by what I needed to do, how to direct my family, and I often forgot how sensitive and open you were to others. I do hope you can forgive my gruffness and how I pushed your sensitivity aside to make room for what I felt needed to be done." A look of sadness came across his face. "You were a reminder of my own shortcomings, and I resented you for that."

Leon shook his head, astonished by his father's straightforwardness. "This isn't at all what I expected when I agreed to this walk. I guess I was still looking for criticism and judgement about how I lived my life. I never once thought forgiveness was a possibility, or even an issue."

Big Dad stopped him. "You did nothing wrong. I was so stubborn and self-absorbed, my treating you with disregard was my shortcoming, not yours. Are you saying you forgive me? I do love you as you are with no exception."

Big tears rolled down Leon's cheeks, and he responded to his father without hesitation. "Thank you for being my dad, and of course I forgive you and ask for yours in return." At that point there was no more exchange of words, only love radiating between the two men.

I say radiating because, truly, it was as though I could *see* love on these family walks whenever words cleared the air between them.

During the walks with Leon, a veil seemed to lift that had been between him and his father all their lives. Big Dad realized that he had been too hard on his first-born son, who had always felt not good enough for his father's love. The reassurance Leon received on the walks, I felt, was very healing for him, as he received the respect from his father that he had not received before.

Once again, communication stripped away misunderstandings and unhelpful expectations, leaving only forgiveness and unconditional love. There was no pretense, only authentic exchanges without the filters we typically use while in our physical bodies.

After Leon's passing, I received a vision of the reunion that took place after he crossed over. Our ancestors welcomed him as the beautiful, loving soul he was. Although Leon had lived in his younger brother's shadow, the light that radiated from his ancestors dissolved that shadow, like flipping a light switch in a dark closet. He was embraced completely and unconditionally. It was a joyous celebration of a soul's continued journey and a soul's innate belonging, no matter what role the person had played in their family.

I've come to understand that sometimes the roles we play create opportunities for others to experience more love and expansion. In order for growth and expansion to occur, we may need to be honest with ourselves about times we've been judgmental and less than loving toward those who are closest to us.

8

Stolen Innocence

"Imagine how different the world would be
if little girls were taught to set boundaries as often
as they are taught to be polite." Hailey Magee

After my walks with Uncle Everett, I had discovered that I could create the space for connecting with others by going into meditation with that intention. I would focus on a family member or another person with whom I was close who was preparing to make his or her transition or going through some kind of trauma.

I focused on Mom's sister Yvonne many times as her health declined, while she was in assisted living. Two years younger than Mom, Yvonne had faced major challenges in the family dynamic and was often referred to as the black sheep. A basketball player in her youth, she had become involved with one of the high school athletic stars. She became pregnant at seventeen, a tragedy in those days, when the advice given girls in our family was "to keep a dime between your knees." It was the only sex education any of us received.

My grandparents sent Yvonne to a group home for unwed mothers to have the baby, then insisted that she give the baby up for adoption. Throughout her life Yvonne carried this deep loss as well as guilt and shame for having gotten pregnant. She blamed herself for destroying the community's perception that the family was perfect.

My grandfather was a church deacon, proud of his standing and the standing of his family as good Christians in the community. This extremely religious family was horrified and painfully embarrassed, my grandfather most of all. When he learned that Yvonne was pregnant, he resigned as deacon, a position he had worked toward all his life. Shame fell heavy over the entire family.

According to stories I heard growing up, Yvonne went the way of the wayward daughter.

After the birth of the baby, she returned home to live with my grandparents, earned her high school GED, and became a secretary at a large company in Lebanon. The next several years were chaotic, as she drank and sought the company of men wherever she could find them. While war maneuvers were being held near Lebanon before World War II, she would disappear for days.

Big Dad didn't know what to do with her. My mother, her siblings, and my grandparents were so embarrassed by Yvonne's behavior that my father moved the family out of Lebanon, the hometown they loved.

During the late 1930's and 1940's, society considered women to be the instigators of men's bad behavior by putting themselves in situations to have sex. Yvonne, like other girls and women during that time, had not been given instructions on what to do with feelings that might arise when she found herself alone with a boy who was aroused by her beauty and personality.

Yvonne was blessed – or cursed – with both, however you want to look at it. The father of her child was a "big man on campus" who could do no wrong and was never held accountable for his actions. It is my belief that he seduced Yvonne against her will. She had no idea what was happening and had sex with him only because she wanted to be accepted and loved.

My walks with Yvonne took place as I sat by her side in an assisted living facility. In the early walks, she had many deep conversations with her parents. The most memorable was when she spoke with her father about the baby. Big Dad was not happy about how he had treated her and how he had handled the situation. He told Yvonne he wished he had been more understanding and not so quick to condemn.

Big Dad looked weary when Yvonne and I first entered the Dome of Light. He didn't know what to expect and said to Yvonne, "It is very good to see you. I wasn't sure you would come after all that happened between us."

He continued, "I want you to hear me when I say I really wish I had reacted differently all those years ago. I know now you were manipulated and became the target for all my suppressed anger and grief. It's probably hard to grasp that I was totally committed to the self- righteous teachings of the church with little room for error or forgiveness. I know I was wrong, and the true teachings of Jesus would not have judged you or punished you as I did.

Big Dad looked her in the eye and said, "Thank you for being open to being here. I hope you feel my love and regret for what happened between us."

Yvonne's face registered shock at what she had just heard. "I expected to grovel at your feet to ask for your forgiveness. Never in my wildest hour did I suspect you felt bad about the way you treated me."

"I am truly sorry," Big Dad said. "I'm grateful we have come together and know our continued journey will be much easier now that we have said our peace and made our amends. I love you."

This was huge for Yvonne. I could see that she was almost dancing with delight at her father's words. I knew she had felt abandoned when she most needed their support.

In fact, after they sent her away, they had refused any contact with her during the pregnancy. Big Dad had discouraged Big Mama from supporting her daughter because of the shadow an illegitimate birth cast over the family. Yvonne's pregnancy and its impact on the family caused her much anguish and emotional struggle throughout her life, including bouts of mental illness. She had lived with many years of shame and regret because of the way life hit her. Later, she did marry but never had another child.

After that particular walk, I was overcome with relief and feelings of peacefulness. My healing tears flowed for her. Yvonne had been carrying this grief and pain around since she was seventeen, more than seventy years.

On a later walk, Yvonne asked about her son. As she made this request, to my surprise a handsome young man in his early forties came forward – her son who was now grown – to thank her for giving birth to him and letting him go to the loving family that adopted him. Yvonne's son had the features of the family, our almost black hair, big blue-green eyes, and a smile that required being returned by those who were smiled upon. Yvonne's son was about six feet tall with a strong build as well.

When he spoke to her, he beamed, "I finally get to see you, I have dreamed of you often, wondering where you were and how you were doing. I just want you to know that I have had a wonderful life with loving parents who would not have been parents if not for your sacrifice.

They provided for me and gave me love as if I was born to them. Please know you did the right thing. All I know is you were an unmarried teen who could not provide for me. What a gift you gave. I know it could not have been easy. Thank you and thank you for loving me that much. We will see each other again and you will recognize me. I'll make sure of it."

After this walk, Yvonne took a deep breath and relaxed in a way I had not seen her do before, the muscles of her face softening and her shoulders relaxing into the bed.

Yvonne made her transition while she was in assisted living. I have continued to walk to visit her from time to time. When I check in today, there is none of the fear, shame, or regret that was present in the early walks. Since her passing, she has reunited with her husband Jerry, who died twenty-five years before she did. He is always present on recent walks I've taken with Yvonne, but he has yet to say anything. He was totally devoted to her. Jerry had gone to her father before they married to assure him how much he loved her and would devote his life to caring for her. That is exactly what he did and according to the final walks with her, he is still lovingly by her side.

NOTES

9

Just Wanted to Make It Right

"Humans are born in truth, but we grow up believing in lies." Don Miquel Ruiz

Memories about my Aunt Doris recently surfaced from when I was a child. She and her family came to visit us every two or three years, and their visits always made my mother anxious. Doris had attended a Christian college, where she met her husband, who later became a Church of Christ preacher and missionary. She worked alongside her husband, spreading the gospel and living their idea of the example of a Christian life. On their visits, she made subtle, veiled comments that were often judgmental of my parents. She clearly did not like that we were allowed to be "normal" kids and often quoted scripture to make her point. Her self-righteousness could not be disguised. Wearing shorts, dancing, and swimming in mixed company were all no- no's according to the religious laws that Doris upheld. I have never been close to her and always felt I was doing something wrong when she was around.

My mother loved her sister but also knew she could not meet Doris's standards. Doris's and her husband's interpretation of the Bible was much narrower than that of the church we attended. I imagine Doris did a great deal of praying for our souls after their visits to our house. I was grateful that the visits became fewer after Doris's family moved to Atlanta, where her husband had been hired as preacher.

"

When my memories resurfaced, Aunt Doris was in her mid-eighties and in poor health. I decided to go into meditation and ask if she would like to walk with me. As I connected with her heart-to-heart, I felt a great deal of fear and asked what that was about. The message I received was that Doris felt that she had not lived a "pure" enough life to enter the Kingdom of Heaven and would have to "pay" in the afterlife for not being a good enough Christian.

As we began our walk, we faced the gallery of the family that had already crossed over. Her mother, father, brothers, my mother, and Otelia stood with many others who greeted us with a glow radiating from the center of their being. Doris and her father, my Big Dad, began to communicate telepathically. It always amazes me that I can understand the communication, although no words are spoken aloud.

Doris was fourteen when Yvonne became pregnant and was sent to the home for unwed mothers. Doris had felt the pain and anguish of her parents and wanted to do something to make everything right again. She had taken the family shame to heart.

Standing before her father in the Dome of Light, Doris was overcome with grief. "I tried as hard as I could to make the family whole again. I prayed and aspired every day to be the perfect Christian so that I could heal the pain and shame you carried. I felt that if I lived the best life I could as a Christian, I could make up for the pain caused by my sister."

Before Big Dad spoke, he looked at Doris with such love. "Oh, my sweet daughter, it was not your burden to bear. I did not handle the crisis the way a loving father should, and I have held that regret for many years. I have learned now to focus on forgiving your sister, but most of all forgiving myself. You have nothing to be ashamed of, nor have you done anything wrong.

The way you lived your life is as it should have been. It's time you forgive yourself and see others with the eyes of God. No more judgments."

Doris wailed. "Daddy, I didn't know you felt such pain and guilt. Of course, I forgive you and accept your love with all my heart."

Doris saw suddenly that she had judged others all her life, and she had done so because of her belief that Yvonne had destroyed the family by committing the unforgiveable sin of getting pregnant out of wedlock. As Doris broke down crying, four-year-old Otelia ran into Doris's arms.

"You are so beautiful," Otelia said with a bright smile. "I've watched how much you love others and have always tried to take care of everybody else."

Big Mama, whose rocking chair suddenly appeared beside Otelia, motioned Doris to sit down in the rocker. Otelia crawled into Doris's lap.

Doris held Otelia tightly as they rocked. "I could have done better. I tried so hard to be the perfect Christian daughter, wife, and mother."

Otelia looked tenderly at Doris. "Your hair is just like our momma's. I used to love to brush her hair. I've been near you as you brushed yours. I bet mine would have been long just like yours and Momma's." She placed her head on Doris's shoulder and touched her cheek to feel the tears. "I love you and I'm so happy you came to visit. I know our poppa feels better, too."

As they rocked, Doris shared thoughts that I was pretty sure no one had heard from her before. "I love my family so much, I can't bear the thought of their being punished for what they did in this life. I really do believe the teachings that if you don't live your best life, you waill spend eternity in hell. It just scares me, and I feel I have to protect my family from themselves."

"I know you're afraid," Otelia said. "I've been watching all my brothers and sisters for a long time. I am never far from you.

"We're happy in this place," she assured Doris. "I know God loves me and all our family.

It's okay to be afraid. When I get afraid, I sing my favorite song, 'Jesus Loves Me.' You can sing it when you're afraid for any of us. It will make you feel better. You don't need to worry. Love is always here."

They sang together and rocked as Otelia took the hairpins out of Doris's hair and began stroking and combing her long grey hair.

I saw that it looked exactly like my grandmother's and knew then that all her life Doris had wanted to be like her mother, who in Doris's eyes was the perfect Christian woman.

As they rocked, Doris began to see scenes from her life where she had been harsh and judged more than she had expressed love. This review awakened a spark of love in her that she had not known was there. She could feel it in her heart, like a little door creaking open.

Otelia seemed to know exactly what Doris was experiencing. "You've done the best you knew to do because you believed you were doing the work of God, just as your father wanted."

When they completed their time together, Otelia quoted the Bible, "Judge not, that you be not judged," and Doris seemed to embrace it.

Before they parted, Doris thanked her family for their love and for the opportunity to talk with her father and Otelia. She returned home to think about her life and how her judgment of others had created so much separation in the family. As Doris and I each reviewed what we had learned on our walk, I felt that both of us needed to do more work on forgiving. It was an "aha" moment for me. I needed to forgive Doris for what I felt she had imposed on me and my family.

One thing was obvious to me. Doris loved us. Belief systems held too tightly can cloud love that has always been there. I believe now that she sincerely feared for our salvation and wanted to make sure we were saved from eternal damnation.

It reminds me of words I refer to often, "When I think I know, I know I don't. There is much more to be considered."

NOTES

10

Born Grieving

"Of course, loss is the great lesson." Mary Oliver

Otelia had passed away while my mother was in utero. Big Mama was grieving the loss of Otelia when Mother was born. From what I can tell, my mother was born grieving, too. There was always a hint of sadness around her. I believe that the family's grief about Otelia's death permeated my mother's infant body and soul.

Few stories have been told about my mother's early years, and no photos exist that I know about or have seen. With the turmoil in the world between the end of WWI and the beginning of the Great Depression, and the tragic loss in my grandparents' lives, it appears that Mom's first years passed without much celebration.

She would become the oldest of five living children. As the oldest, she was often responsible for her siblings. While I was growing up, I heard more stories about the boys since Mom was often their caregiver. She did the best she could to make sure they got ready for church on time and stayed out of trouble. Of course, the boys loved to aggravate her, such as getting in the tree next to the road and hiding from her when it was time to go to church. All of her siblings liked to tease her, especially when she started to date my dad.

Leon and Everett passed away before Mother and her sisters. My mother could not understand why she was still alive while losing the brothers she had taken care of as children. I believe this took a

51

toll on her. She began to fall often and would lose her way while driving. She didn't care much about what she ate or how she kept the house, which was a dramatic change in her behavior. In 2008, a year after Everett passed, she made the decision at eighty-two to sell her home and car and move into assisted living. It was a good decision for her, and my brothers and I were blessed that she made the decision herself.

Sitting with my mom during her stay in the assisted living facility, I would set an intention to connect with her when she was resting. Several times I asked silently if she would like to see what was on the other side, just for a "visit," and she would usually agree. I always assured her that it was her choice whether to go on the walks, as well as whether to leave her body and move on. I told her that she was the one in control.

Once she agreed, as had happened with my uncles, we found ourselves in the Light Dome facing the ancestors. I could not make out who some of them were, but they radiated love and kindness. Once, we recognized Aunt Essie, my grandfather's sister, by her mink shawl that she had worn every Sunday, even in summer. Many of these ancestors I had never met, and Mom explained who they were. Otelia would be standing between Big Mama and Big Dad or sitting on Big Mama's lap or on Big Dad's shoulders. My uncles, Everett and Leon, were always nearby. On these visits Mom and her loved ones had many loving, telepathic conversations and shared a great deal of laughter.

On one of the first trips, shortly after she had moved into assisted living, she visited with Everett. When we entered the Dome of Light, she was surprised to see her mother, father, Otelia, and Everett. After some hesitation Mom found her voice and relayed how much she missed Everett and that she was grateful to see him so happy and vibrant.

On another walk, Mother and I visited with Robert, a boyfriend she'd had right after high school, before she married Dad. They had dated while my dad was away at college. Mother loved to dance, and that year they attended a dance featuring big band music every Saturday night. For a small town in middle Tennessee, this was "big stuff."

The romance ended when my dad was called home after his freshman year in college due to his father's illness. Mom and Dad had been dating seriously when he left for college but they agreed to see other people while he was gone. On his return they became more serious again and committed to one another.

On their walk, my mother and Robert talked about how much fun they had had together, how neither of them had regrets about going their separate ways. They were both grateful for knowing that they would always be the best of friends.

I had no knowledge of any of this prior to our walk, but later I asked Mom a few questions about life before Dad, and she corroborated much of what I had seen in the vision. She spoke about Robert fondly, about how much fun they'd had together, the way I had seen them reminisce on the walk.

When we spoke of Robert later she reminisced, "He was a fantastic dancer. Oh! What fun we had."

One of the most awesome experiences with Mom was when we met with her mother, my grandmother. In this walk, Big Mama appeared very clear and solid, while the others who were present were somewhat faded. This was usually a clue to me that the conversation would be of special importance. Otelia was sitting on Big Mama's knee in her rocking chair, and Mom sat on a stool at Big Mama's feet. This session was different from other visits where Mom and I stood side by side holding hands, facing the ancestors.

Big Mama took a deep breath and sighed. "My, you are such a brave woman! After all that we have been through together, you still radiate affection and appreciation from every cell of your being."

Mom's face lit up, apparently surprised and pleased.

"When I first discovered I was pregnant, after Otelia passed," Big Mama stroked Otelia's fine hair, "I didn't know how I would handle the grief and the joy I felt all at once. The void you filled was tremendous, and I always felt I had placed the burden of my grief on your tiny shoulders. Please forgive me."

Mom was astonished. "It was a beautiful life having you as my mother, just the way you are. Most of our days were filled with laughter and joy. The sad days were always transformed by old stories that added a drop of humor to our days. I loved that we ended up laughing and crying at the same time. And I knew we were both grateful for each other. I wouldn't have wanted it any different."

Big Mama shook her head, "You carried the grief like a badge of honor, but I know you've also carried it throughout your life, suffering your own losses and disappointments."

"It's true." Mom nodded. "There have been plenty of losses. But I never blamed anything on you."

"You are my true daughter," Big Mama said. "I'll always cherish our life together."

On this visit, Otelia, my mother, and I connected on a deeper level than on any of the other walks. My mother and Otelia acknowledged my presence and thanked me for my love and the grace that brought all of us together. My relationship with Otelia continued to grow and become stronger as I took more family members to experience the other side. The more I observed Otelia and the more our connection deepened, I realized even more deeply that I am Otelia incarnated in this lifetime. It became clearer that she is my connection to those who have passed over. I began to understand that there is so much more than we can possibly know while living on this Earth plane.

The conversation between Mom and her father, Big Dad, is one of the most memorable exchanges in my experience of the walks. It is what I have come to call *the* conversation.

When we first entered the Dome of Light, Big Dad motioned my mother forward as he took a seat on steps I hadn't noticed before. Mother joined him on the step below, where she sat looking up at him, waiting for him to speak.

Big Dad smiled broadly at my mother and spoke affectionately. "Oh, how I have missed you being in my presence. I've dreamed of having this opportunity to tell you how grateful I am for you and all you did to help Big Mama and me through some of the hardest years of our lives. If you had not been born when you were, I do not know how my precious wife would have made it through the loss of our Otelia.

"From the time you were born, you helped alleviate the grief, and I now know that it cost you dearly. I am eternally grateful to you not only for helping us through that grief but also being strong when the family fell apart after Yvonne's transgression. Although you've had your own life's traumas, you were the anchor for our family when no one else could have carried the burden."

Mother paused, considering his words. "The only thing for me to say is that I just did what you taught me to do. I felt I was always supported. Even in my darkest hours, I never felt alone. Call it what you want, but you were always there giving me strength wherever I went and whatever happened. How we all reacted to Yvonne's situation was just what we did. Thank you for opening the Dome of Light so that we could have these conversations. It has made the bonds among us stronger. I'm filled with forgiveness, admiration, and respect for all that this family has been through."

This was how I learned that Big Dad was the one responsible for the Dome of Light that allowed my family to engage with those they loved and come to greater understanding and peace.

"Not good enough" was a common theme in many of my family's conversations. During their time on the planet, they had apparently rarely spoken about this feeling, but on their walks, no one pretended otherwise or hedged the issue. I was often surprised at the level of honesty and authenticity in the conversations that occurred within the Dome of Light.

When I was growing up, my experience of Big Dad was of a brusque man who was hard to get close to. During the walks, I learned that Mother had felt the same way. On one of the walks, again sitting on the steps, feeling inadequate was the topic that dominated their conversation.

Mom opened up first. "I hear that you were – and are – grateful for my presence after Otelia's death. But the truth is that I didn't feel like I had your approval growing up. You always seemed distant and preoccupied. I don't remember ever hearing you say anything complementary or positive about what I did. There was always the air around our conversations that you felt I could have done more, and better."

My grandfather seemed stunned. He choked up. "That was never how I felt! You were a ray of sunshine in my life. I was so grateful you came along when you did. Your mother and I were so blessed to have another beautiful daughter. After losing Otelia as we did, I guess I carried the fear that something would happen to you. I feared I was not a good enough husband, father, or provider to fill the shoes God had given me. It seems that theme carried into your heart, too. I am so sorry."

He breathed deeply, closing his eyes for a moment. When he opened them again, he looked intently into my mother's eyes. "I wanted to be the best father to you that I possibly could. When I look back now, I see that I shut down my emotions. I carried unresolved grief about Otelia that I barricaded behind a stone wall to protect me from feeling the depth of my pain. My anger was never toward you. My anger with God about Otelia's death is what stifled my love for you and all my children."

After this exchange, both of their faces relaxed into a kind of radiance I had not seen on either of them before. They stood up from their places on the steps and, although they didn't touch, I felt an energetic connection between them, a connection of reconciliation and acceptance.

When I opened my eyes and glanced at Mom in the bed beside me, she took a long, deep breath, and her body softened into the bed. An expression of peace flooded her face as she rested. I believe it was an important awareness for both of us that Big Dad had been a devoted father and grandfather, with unconditional love for his children and grandchildren.

Mother had always felt that he was angry with her. She didn't understand this and tried, even after his death, to get his approval. I believe that his sharing of what was really going on with him helped her to find love and compassion for him on a much deeper level.

I never talked about these walks and visions with Mom, but she seemed to know at some level. After each walk, when I'd open my eyes, she would say, "I am so glad you are here. What would I do without my beautiful daughter?"

She had a hard time accepting that she was good enough for heaven, which we talked about after one of the walks.

"How many times have you asked Jesus for forgiveness?" I asked. "Every day."

"And does he tell you he forgives you?"

Mother nodded positively

"Well, do you believe him, or not?"

"Mom gave me an exasperated look. "Oh, Jill!"

***

Among the most powerful and memorable walks with my mother were those when she connected with my dad. They had been high school sweethearts. As football captain, he escorted my mother, the homecoming queen, to homecoming festivities. They courted for several years, dating other people but always coming back to each other. Dad was a hunter who owned hunting dogs as a teenager, which he loved. I'd seen several pictures of them in the country with his big black-and-white retriever, which I imagined was walking and playing around them. Visiting with their individual families was also a major part of their dating time. Mother's house was always full of relatives, so I imagine they went to Dad's home for peace and quiet.

They were married in February 1942, and on their honeymoon Mom became pregnant with Wayne. Dad was drafted into the Coast Guard and had to leave Mom with her parents for several months. After his basic training he was stationed in Miami, where she eventually joined him. We always kidded him about "guarding" the beach. After the war, they returned to Tennessee to start their life together. John was born three years later, then shortly came me, Barbara Jill. In five more years, Jake surprised us all.

When Dad was diagnosed with a rare blood disease at age thirty-four, there were four children at home between the ages of two and thirteen. Because of his disease, he could not get life insurance. He worried constantly about what would happen when he died and often used alcohol to escape his pain. Feelings of guilt and shame carried him deeper into despair. I learned on the walks that these

58

feelings had worsened when he died and left Mom, a widow at forty-five with two young children still at home.

Mom had a difficult time holding the household together financially and emotionally, both during his illness and after he passed. During their walks, Dad apologized for leaving her with all the responsibilities of raising their children and holding the house together. He was proud of the way she had moved forward with her life, never giving up the family values of acceptance and responsibility for each other no matter what hardships she faced. He knew that it had been a hard journey and that she had done it bravely. Dad wanted Mom to know how much he loved her. It was an emotional exchange, one that moved me deeply. As many times before, I found myself in tears – not tears of sorrow, but of joy.

As they stood looking at each other, openly grateful to be in each other's presence, Dad said, "Seeing you is the answer to many prayers I've said in the past. Leaving you to endure life without me was the hardest part about leaving my broken and diseased form. I hope you know I held on as long as I could, even knowing that watching me suffer was very difficult for you to bear. I just knew I would come home to you again."

Mom took in his words. "I watched you suffer as much as I could manage. Although I didn't want you to leave, I wanted your suffering to end. You gave me the courage I needed to move forward. You always believed in my inner strength even when I didn't."

"That's the woman I have always loved," Dad spoke with a gleam in his eye I remembered seeing often. "Know I have been watching over you as you've gone through the joyful and trying times of your life. We had and always will have that special bond."

Dad's words gave Mom another opportunity to speak her heart. "I always felt I wasn't good enough for the love you showed to me.

I thought bearing your children and making a home for all of you was my greatest responsibility. It was my way of expressing love. All those times you needed a hug and I was too busy, I am sorry. Although I know I did provide a loving home, as I saw it, I forgot that being your wife was the most important job of all." Mom's eyes seem to warm as she said, "You are my sunshine, and always will be."

"You Are My Sunshine" was their song. They often talked about how they had harmonized as they drove to their honeymoon location. It eventually became the family song that we sang on road trips. Mom wanted it sung at her funeral, too. A couple who knew both Mom and Dad harmonized the song just for her. Not a dry eye!

I felt that much pain and grief were released during their conversations. Dad asked for forgiveness, apologizing for not being the man he believed Mom deserved. He had grown up in a blue-collar family, his father working for the railroads and his mother a clerk in a shoe store. For the majority of their marriage, my dad sold produce to grocery stores, which was an embarrassment for him. He had wanted to offer much more.

Hearing this gave Mom a chance to receive him in an entirely different way. She acknowledged what had happened and took responsibility for putting more energy into being a homemaker and mother than into being a wife.

From the time Dad was diagnosed, Mom held up as best she could, but she became more distant from Dad. Sometimes when he hugged or affectionately embraced her, she would push him away and say, "Stop that!" in a dismissive tone although she tried to be kidding. She did what she believed was her job to take care of the family and make the most peaceful home she could, while Dad retreated into his woodworking shop and drank alone.

A year before his passing, when Dad joined Alcoholics Anonymous, Mom attended AL Anon meetings. This brought them closer together and helped Mom cope with his worsening condition and death. On the walks they acknowledged how grateful they were for that time they shared. The sound of the laughter and giggles I had often heard from behind the closed door of their bedroom filled the Dome of Light. The closeness they felt again as Dad neared his passing was a treasure they shared and reminisced about during the walks.

Two years later, after she moved into the assisted living facility called the Manor, Mother's primary care physician prescribed Aricept, a new drug intended to slow the progression of dementia. As soon as she started taking the drug, she began declining both physically and mentally. By November 2010, she had become more feeble and less active. In early December she was admitted to the hospital with a grand mal seizure and sepsis. She had several more seizures and the sepsis continued, so she was moved to a rehab facility for treatment. When she was able to return to the Manor, she was moved into the extended care wing.

Over the next few months, she continued to decline. Her energy never returned. My brothers and I hired sitters during the day, and I stayed with her most nights. During these visits, she and I took many walks, and I became closer to her than ever before. We giggled a great deal for no apparent reason. Her congestive heart failure continued to progress, and by the end of April she was in such a weakened state that Hospice was called in to take over her care. In extended care, the family was required to administer morphine by mouth since no nurses were on duty during the night. My brothers came to help out and be near her.

Around 5:30 on the morning of May 6, I administered a dose of morphine and looked into her eyes, which were even more hollow than I'd seen before and sunken into her head. I was overwhelmed by her look of complete helplessness, and I knew she was asking for my help.

Standing by her bedside, touching her forehead, I said, "Enough already!" and with as much love as I could muster, "Okay, that's enough. You have lived a good life, and this body has served you well. All those you have loved that have passed over are here now to greet you: Dad, Big Mama, Big Dad, Everett, Otelia, and all the rest."

I kissed her on the forehead. "I'm going to get a cup of coffee. If you choose to leave with them while I'm gone, that's perfect. We will always be connected by love, and that love will never go away. You think you're ever going to get rid of me?"

We both smiled, and I left the room. When I returned 15 minutes later, there was a look of deep peace on her face. She had left her body just moments before. I was extremely grateful. She passed the Friday before Mother's Day. We held her visitation on Mother's Day. Very appropriate from my point of view.

Shortly after Mom passed, I attended a Celebration of Life gathering at Canyon Lake, Texas, for a dear friend's wife. There was food and wine with music and singing on a huge deck overlooking the lake. Three musicians sang folk songs and spiritual favorites while others played guitars and a fiddle. It was a clear night in late June with the stars glimmering and the moon dancing on the water. A cool summer breeze embraced the celebration.

I was still grieving, and my thoughts drifted to Mom. As I sipped wine, I looked up and in my mind's eye saw Mom and Dad, dressed as they were in photos from when they were courting at Lebanon High School. Mother wore a white blouse with a black tie pinned at the neck and an ankle-length, flowing black skirt, bobby socks, and saddle oxfords. Dad was in dark slacks, white T-shirt, and his football lettermen's jacket. He sat on the upper step with Mom on his lap as they listened to the music. They looked over at me and smiled the biggest smiles ever. I began crying and totally lost any semblance of composure.

It is the most beautiful thing I have ever experienced.

11

Bluebonnets and Butterflies

*"There are two ways to live your life.
One is as though nothing is a miracle.
The other is as though everything
is a miracle." Albert Einstein*

After Mom passed, I felt restless. I was free of family responsibilities for the first time in my life. I could go anywhere and do anything. Thinking I was going to settle near friends in Austin, Texas, I packed my belongings in Murfreesboro, Tennessee, put them on a moving van, and sent them to Austin, where they were stored. This, I thought, would begin my new adventure. I often say, "I ran away from home."

However, it didn't exactly work out the way I hoped. A new home in Austin did not materialize. I rented a room for a month, spent six weeks housesitting in Sedona, Arizona, then traveled back east to spend the holidays with family in Asheville, North Carolina. By the time I returned to Texas in January 2012, I was exhausted and ready to settle down somewhere, anywhere.

While asking if anyone knew of a place to rent in Austin, Canyon Lake, or San Antonio at a reasonable cost, the name Rebecca Rodriguez kept coming up in conversations. I learned that Rebecca was a realtor who was well-connected and knew the area.

One Sunday afternoon while I was attending a workshop to learn about a particular type of healing, my friend Sydney introduced me to Rebecca, who smiled warmly upon meeting me. Rebecca had short, reddish-brown hair and dancing blue eyes that sparkled as she spoke. I was drawn to her immediately.

"Rebecca, I feel I'm supposed to ask you about a place to live in Canyon Lake or Austin," I told her.

She studied me for a moment, then said, "How would you like to stay in my place at Canyon Lake? I'm leaving on Thursday for Santa Fe and will be gone for three months. I hadn't thought about a house sitter, but that feels like a good idea. When can you come out and see if this will work for you?"

It was settled in the first two minutes of our meeting. On my visit two days later, we discussed the details of my moving in on the coming Saturday.

The home and property were stunning. Every window had a view of Canyon Lake, and overlooking the lake was a full-sized wooden labyrinth with a large rose quartz at the center. In addition to house sitting, I was to take care of two cats that had been on the property for many years: Miss Kitty, an eight-year-old, black-and-white tabby who came around only at mealtime or to see who was walking the labyrinth, and a fourteen-year-old grey male named Whiskers, also known as Whiskey. Rebecca told me that Whiskey did not want to be bothered or touched.

As it turned out, Whiskey wanted to be close to me all the time. He was an outdoor cat who quickly became an indoor one. I made him as comfortable as possible, while taking care to protect the floors and home furnishings. I bought a throw especially for him that I placed next to me wherever I sat and put a litter box in the house. Over the next eighteen months, we became close buddies.

The Canyon Lake property, which Rebecca owned with her partner Nancy, turned out to be an ideal place for me to go through the grieving process about my mom, and Whiskey was with me through it all. He walked the labyrinth with me, and when I walked too fast, he would lie down on the path in front of me. If I tried to step over him, he would swipe at me with his claws. We spent many peaceful hours together. I was healing from losing my mom, and he was ending his days in his body. Mostly we just thought of butterflies and sunshine. Me, because my mom loved butterflies.

The following summer Rebecca rented out the main house and I stayed in what was called the boathouse – a storage structure converted into a bedroom, bathroom, and small living area with a screened-in porch overlooking the labyrinth. Whiskey and I loved this space, but after the summer we moved back into the main house, happy the renters were gone.

A year later, Rebecca decided to sell her home and move to Santa Fe permanently. After the house sold, it became obvious that Whiskey would not relocate without trauma. I could tell he was quite ill, probably with cancer. As the day of my move drew nearer, he became more lethargic and stayed in the corner of whatever room I was in. We dreamed about walking together through sunshine meadows and snoozed in the shade of the large trees by the lake. He was very satisfied with the property, and his rubbing my legs and looking up at me let me know without a doubt he was not going to leave. I could also feel he was in significant pain and was ready to leave his body. Rebecca and I decided that on the day of my move, she would take him to the vet. As the only one who could pick him up, I placed him in the carrier for his journey.

Later that day, when I was sitting outside thinking of him and how much I loved and appreciated his presence in my life, his image appeared before me as a strong and healthy young cat. He looked me directly in the eyes and thanked me for making his final years comfortable and full of love. He told me I was his favorite human.

I saw him playing in flowers, mainly bluebonnets, with butterflies flitting about. This was a special image for me. My mom loved butterflies, and I had healed so much during my eighteen-month stay in the Canyon Lake house. It was a sacred space. In the past, Rebecca had done many workshops focusing on the labyrinth and the goddess energy around the lake. Alone with just Whiskey and Miss Kitty, it had been safe to laugh, cry, dance, or do whatever I needed to do to celebrate my mom and our life together.

It was a "God thing" that landed me at Canyon Lake, clearly orchestrated at a level beyond my own doing. When I arrived, it had been only six months since my mom's passing. She had been central in my life since my divorce twenty-four years earlier. While at the lake house, Whiskey and I walked the labyrinth often. I would cry and laugh about Mom's life and her death, enjoying the solitude the space granted me. I'll always be grateful for the gift of the Canyon Lake house and the time to grieve my mom's passing. I had come to a place of love and joy that our lives together had given us both. And Whiskey had been my constant support and companion.

Thank you, Whiskey, Rebecca, and Nancy for such a sacred gift.

12

Kuan Yin's Blessing

*"Everything in the Universe is connected.
Within each it is reflected." Lourdes Pita*

After Uncle Everett passed, I shared the story of our walks with his daughter and with my mother, both of whom understood and accepted the visions. Each time I told the story, I remembered more about the walks, which opened me to the possibility of walking with Uncle Leon, my mom, Aunt Yvonne, Aunt Doris, and my ex-husband Stan. Each experience taught me more about holding the space for souls to explore possibilities of what awaits them after they make their transition or as they struggle with decisions about the next step on their journey.

It can be very difficult for the person who feels they have unfinished business or is worried about leaving their loved ones behind. Most I have walked with believe this lifetime is the only chance they have to get it right. The struggle to remain in form almost always takes over. Even when the body is done, the will to live becomes very powerful. Some say this is the ego-mind whose job it is to make sure the form survives.

I believe that the connections my family members and I made on these walks have relieved much worry and stress for those who are going through trauma or facing serious health issues, if only on a subconscious level. Knowing what *is* has given all of us the gift of peace.

This was shown to me most profoundly when I took a walk with Susan, three years after my mom's passing.

I knew Susan through our mutual friend Sydney. They had grown up together and had shared many adventures. When Susan began to show symptoms of Huntington's disease in her late fifties, losing the ability to swallow and having difficulty speaking, Sydney and I started a practice of sending love to her on a regular basis.

As the disease progressed, Susan lost a lot of weight and became reclusive. Friends and family were deeply concerned, but Susan made it known she wanted no intervention. During the last two years of her life, her health diminished steadily, finally requiring a feeding tube and constant care. Near the end, she was placed in the ICU and intubated. Sydney traveled to Sugarland, Texas, to be at Susan's bedside, and I joined her to offer prayers and hold the space for what might occur as Susan neared death. We felt she was hanging on for her older daughter, Sarah, to arrive from North Carolina.

While sitting in the ICU with some of Susan's friends and her younger daughter, Ami, I asked in meditation from my heart to Susan's if there was anything she would like to do outside the body. As I always do, I assured Susan that she was in charge and could come back into the body at any time.

Immediately, Susan said she was excited to have the chance to walk her dogs, something she loved to do and used to do at least twice daily. My vision took us to a homey neighborhood of pristine yards with older trees and welcoming landscapes where we walked two frisky, well- groomed labs, one white and one black, which in my vision were completely dedicated to Susan. The dogs were young, and so was she. Susan had a smile on her face and a bounce in her step.

Back in the ICU, I observed Susan's light body looking down at her physical body in the bed, which was struggling to breathe. I knew it was Susan in the column of light because of her distinctive posture: she stood very straight even when her body was so malnourished and weak, radiating an aura of strength even in her weakened condition. At the same time that she was observing her physical form, an etheric form of her dogs jumped onto the hospital bed and snuggled next to her, one on each side. I found out later that her two labs, one white and one black, had slept that way with her each night.

Over the next few days, as I continued to sit with Susan in meditation, I saw and felt her beautiful essence and sent prayers of "enough suffering," assuring her that she could let go whenever she was ready. This was all taking place leading up to Mother's Day, exactly three years to the day after Mom's passing. It was surreal for me. I experienced many flashbacks to my mom's dying process, and I felt her presence the entire time I was focused on Susan.

After the first walk to the other side with Susan, we continued to walk the dogs often.

Each time the dogs became younger, and so did she. Late in the day before she passed, we took another walk. This time we ended on her deck watching the dogs play in a small yard, as she and I drank glasses of wine. She appeared to be very peaceful.

Amado, her estranged husband of ten years, joined her with his own glass of wine and asked forgiveness for letting her down and not being the husband she deserved. He told her he loved her and expressed remorse for his shortcomings as a father and husband. Susan reassured him that they had let each other down, and that had not diminished their love for each other.

They both expressed gratitude and understanding that they had done the best they knew to do and that everything turned out perfect in the end. They laughed about when they first met, their beautiful daughters, and the love they still feel for one another. They spoke of swim meets and camping trips, things I had no way of knowing about.

Shortly after this experience, Sydney told me that while she prayed, she had asked Amado to come. This was at the same time he had appeared in my vision.

As Susan continued to weaken, the hospital withdrew efforts to keep her alive, providing only what was necessary to keep her comfortable. The family waited by her bedside.

On Saturday, the day before Mother's Day, Sydney and I decided to go for lunch at a restaurant away from the hospital, one that was close to a Buddhist temple dedicated to Kuan Yin, a master in Buddhist teachings. In front of the temple a statue of Kuan Yin stands seventy- two feet high, visible from several blocks away, above the trees and rooftops.

Sydney and I are both drawn to Kuan Yin, partly because of the story of Kuan Yin's decision to stay in the heavens around earth to teach compassion and hold all children in safety. The first time I saw this statue I fell to my knees. Nothing like that had ever happened to me before. In white pants even!

The site is sacred and significant for me on many levels, especially because of a dream I'd had twenty years previously. In my late thirties and going through a divorce, before I began to explore spirituality, I had a vivid dream that introduced me to Kuan Yin. It was a rough and sad year, filled with change, heartbreak, and a sense of failure and shame. As sometimes happens to people during times of difficulty, a dream comes to offer solace.

In the dream I was in an Asian country with half a dozen devotees on the bank of a swollen stream. I was native to this country, and Asian like the other devotees. On the far side of the stream was a huge female deity floating above the surface of the water. She was glowing with love! She was several feet taller than humans, in a flowing white dress of many filmy layers. Her hair was in a bun on the top of her head, and a string of colorful stones circled her hair and fell onto her forehead. She held her hands palms up and open to the sky. Without speaking, she directed us to place ourselves at the edge of the water to catch young children who had been swept away by the rushing water. I sensed they had come from a nearby orphanage, and we were their caregivers. Kuan Yin flooded the area with ropes of light to make sure we were safe while rescuing the children. There were perhaps twenty children, four or five years old.

After the rescue, Kuan Yin bathed us in warming light as we celebrated the rescue. We expressed great joy and gratitude for the beautiful deity that had made it possible. The children were ecstatic, hugging everyone and jumping around gleefully with much laughter and giggles.

When I awoke, I felt I had been blessed, a feeling that sustained me during that dark year.

The dream helped me find peace in knowing that everything was going to work out for my son and me. It was several years later before I was introduced to the spiritual master Kuan Yin, during a workshop I attended in Asheville, North Carolina. When I saw images and read about her, I knew her immediately as the deity from my dream. Since then, I have honored her presence every day by lighting a candle in my home next to a two-foot statue of her. I feel strongly that she continues to surround me in the light I experienced in the dream. I have learned that she brought compassion and affection to support teachers and children, along with much light to the planet.

While writing down the dream in the 1990's, I remembered almost drowning in a swimming pool when I was five. It was a rare family outing that I had looked forward to for weeks. Of course, as a young child, it could have been just days! While floating in the pool in an inner tube near my dad, I decided to slip out of the tube and swim under water to surprise him, but he was further away than I thought. I struggled to reach him and didn't know how to get to the surface. In an instant, hands grabbed me around the waist and lifted me to the surface. It was the lifeguard who had been standing at least thirty feet away. The pool was crowded, but he had seen me go under and knew I was in trouble before my dad even knew I was out of the tube.

It was a scary moment, but all was well. That incident taught me that I will be okay, no matter what happens, a knowing that has served me in many situations. Later, after I'd learned about Kuan Yin, I realized that I was one of the children in the dream. I, too, had been saved.

Sydney and I talked through lunch and decided to drive to the nearby temple to pray for Kuan Yin's assistance in helping Susan cross over. As we entered the grounds, we saw a parking guard directing traffic. This was unusual since other times we had visited the temple, we were the only one present.

We were stunned by what greeted us. The temple grounds had been decorated in brightly painted lotus flowers, and all the porcelain statues had been polished to a brilliant shine. The occasion was the Buddha's birthday, May 21st, which is celebrated the entire month of May.

Our offering of white roses joined with many other offerings of flowers and fruit. We asked for Kuan Yin's assistance and love for Susan during her transition and then walked the grounds feeling grateful to be at the temple during this time of celebration and listening to the festive Vietnamese music being broadcast from the temple. We both knew it was time to get back to Susan, although we would have happily stayed much longer.

About thirty minutes after we returned from the temple, Susan took her last breath. As family and friends gathered around her, I stood nearby, sending devotion and assurances that her daughters would be fine and that the connection between them and their mother would always be present. The girls would have Mother's Day to celebrate her life and not be in the hospital watching her suffer. Susan had given Sarah and Ami that gift.

The full moon in May is considered the birthday of the Buddha, the day he reached enlightenment, and the day he ascended to the heavens—all three events—and is called Wesak. Susan's memorial service was held on the Wesak full moon, bestowing a wave of adoration for her to ride to her next experience.

NOTES

13

Step into Your Own Shoes

"There are a thousand ways to kneel
and kiss the ground." Rumi

Soon after Susan made her transition, I returned to my home in San Antonio. My friend Deanna flew from Tennessee to attend a workshop in Houston and visit me in San Antonio. Her husband David had had major heart issues for several years, as well as symptoms of Hepatitis C. Just weeks before Deanna was scheduled to come to Texas, David had bypass surgery, which did not resolve his heart issues. At the time of her trip, David was in intensive care on a respirator in an induced coma. His doctors encouraged her to go, assuring her that David would be fine until her return and only needed time to recuperate. She reluctantly left him to come to Texas.

I spoke with Deanna while she was enroute, then went into meditation and connected with David in the way that had become familiar to me. I didn't know David well, only as the husband of my friend. I asked if he would like to do anything outside of his body while his body healed.

Immediately we were in a magical place: a peaceful green forest with a slow-moving brook meandering through. David decided to sit beside the brook on a mossy rock. Usually, I stand beside the person who is taking the walk, but this time I was looking on, being present for whatever he needed. David began to talk with what I assumed was an angel or guide, asking for guidance about what he should do.

Deanna and David had chased doctors all over the planet, seeking answers that never seemed to come, so I was not surprised when I heard a voice say, "It is your choice, and only you can make it. You must stop relying on others for your life force and step into your own shoes.

You can fill them. You just have to do it."

I saw the shoes and David standing up ready to put them on. The shoes were large, and David was a small man. It seemed that it was time for David to see and feel himself as big enough, adequate enough, to make decisions for himself. In that instant I was back in my meditation chair.

During Deanna's visit to Texas, we both had a strong sense that he was not going to recover and was choosing to leave his body. When I connected with David again, he asked me to convey to Deanna that he needed her to connect to his heart, without any conversation or intention, just to feel his love for her and hers for him. That was all he was asking from her.

After Deanna returned to Tennessee, the doctors called her to tell her that David had taken a turn for the worse and was not expected to survive much longer. During David's last days, Deanna did what David had asked. She stayed focused on her heart and connected with him heart-to-heart. No drama, no interference, just remaining in the heart energy.

Deanna told him repeatedly, "You are at peace, David. You are truly loved, and my love goes with you into the next phase of your soul's journey."

David passed peacefully while they were alone.

"Nothing but love is real" was the thought she held onto through her grief and the activities of the days that followed.

Deanna and I were sister travelers, studying spiritual teachings and healing modalities, sometimes together and often sharing our experiences. When her daughter Mindy was diagnosed with breast cancer, Deanna brought her to Houston to a well-known cancer clinic. I drove over from San Antonio and took them both to see the Kuan Yin temple in Sugarland. During that time Mindy received a blessing she believed came from Kuan Yin. Mindy felt light surround herself, which she was not expecting since her belief system didn't include the energetic world of healing that her mother and I believe in.

After the visit, Deanna told me that Mindy had become more open to deeper discussions about what is possible beyond the material world. Mindy had never been drawn to her mom's spiritual work and often turned away from her when she tried to help, much like many mother/daughter relationships. After Mindy's experience at the Kuan Yin Temple, the two of them began to experience a more loving relationship. Kuan Yin did her thing, again!

In 2022, Deanna also made her transition after two years battling breast cancer. She was an amazing woman, mother, dedicated healer, and loving friend. I miss her.

NOTES

14

A Friend's Influence

"Nothing among human things has much power to keep our gaze fixed ever more intensely upon God than friendship." Simone Weil

In 2004, when Mom had a heart attack and needed assistance but wasn't ready for assisted living, it was an easy decision for me to retire early from my job with the State of Tennessee, but it took some time to sell my town home in Nashville and move in with her. I had not lived in my hometown of Murfreesboro since I graduated from college in 1973.

I had not kept in touch with most of my high school and college friends, so in a way I was starting over. I had acquaintances but no close friends until I ran into Amanda at a shop in town. I was leaving just as she was entering. Her mother had been my first-grade teacher, and she had graduated from high school with my brother John. We had both lived away from Murfreesboro for many years and we quickly became close friends.

Amanda loved animals. She had five dogs and two cats and had become an animal communicator, able to tell you what an animal was thinking or needed. She worked with horses, cats, dogs, and other animals that were in pain or making their transition.

We spent a great deal of time in her family's country home with her animals. We drank wine and solved the problems of the world. The more time we spent together, I realized how much company a

"

dog would be for me. It was a huge adjustment living back in my hometown, being retired, and spending most of my time with Mom, and it seemed to me that a dog would be a wonderful companion.

With Amanda's encouragement and her promise to mentor me on how to take care of a pet, I adopted a dog named Charlie. I saw photos of him on an adoption site and felt immediately that he and I belonged together. Charlie was a twenty-five pound, yellow-and-white dog with a perfect brown heart on his side. He was beautiful and sweet, too. Without researching his background or his health issues, I welcomed him into my home.

Six weeks after I rescued him, I was dismayed to learn that Charlie suffered from seizures. This I discovered at 2:00 a.m. when he had a seizure under my bed. It sounded like there was more than one dog flopping and whining as though something had a hold of them.

Thus began what seemed like endless visits to a veterinarian, starting with two per week, then dropping to once every two weeks. Charlie not only had nerve damage, which was the cause of the seizures, he also suffered from hip dysplasia that caused him major pain and difficulty eliminating.

He loved to lie next to me when I was meditating and often "traveled" on the walks with me. While we meditated together, he began to show me his ideal life of chasing rabbits in meadows and curling up for naps near babbling brooks. He was always healthy and vibrant on our walks.

In less than a year, Charlie's health deteriorated and visits to the vet became increasingly expensive, including visits to a specialist for his hip issue. Amanda was a tremendous support during this time. She taught me how to massage his hips to relieve some of the pain. The more he was present while I meditated, the more he let me know he wanted out of his body and needed my help. In addition to the pain, he didn't like the way the medications made him feel.

I consulted with Amanda, and after spending time with Charlie, she validated what I was hearing from Charlie. So, after 15 months of watching him suffer, I became convinced Charlie was ready to leave his body. I made an appointment with the veterinarian. Anyone who has had this experience knows that this can be a sad and difficult day.

While sitting in the parking lot waiting for the last patient to leave so that we would have privacy, I asked Charlie to give me a sign that this was really what he wanted me to do. Truly, I did not want to do this. He was lying in the passenger seat next to me. When I asked for a sign, he sat up, looked directly into my face, and winked.

Oh boy! I asked, "Are you sure?"

He came even closer to my face and winked again. I had asked for a sign, and he had given me one.

It was clear what he needed from me. Although it was very hard to participate in ending his life in that particular dog body, he keeps coming to me in meditation and in dreams, playing in meadows and enjoying his new healthy light body. After he died, I drove Charlie to Amanda's farm, where she had created a resting place for her animals. We laid him to rest there, under the watch and care of a statue of St. Francis of Assisi.

Over the next ten years, Amanda and I remained close friends. After Mom passed away and I moved to Texas, I would stay with her when I returned to Tennessee for work or visits. She even had a room fixed up for me. When I moved back to Tennessee in 2016, we picked up our friendship as though I had never left. After a short stay in Murfreesboro and then a move into a condo near Nashville, we talked nearly every day and had lunch or dinner when we could.

Imagine my shock, when on the morning of June 1, 2021, I opened my FaceBook page as usual to a post that jumped off the page: "Amanda Oliver – She will be missed – RIP"

What the hell? I had just spoken with her the day before! *This can't be,* I thought. *It has to be a mistake!*

Amanda had, in fact, suffered a massive brain aneurysm and was in the hospital without brain function. She was clinging to life twenty-four hours after life support had been removed. I learned from one of her friends that Amanda was not expected to recover, but I could get into the ICU to see her one last time to say goodbye.

In Amanda's hospital room, I found three of Amanda's friends sitting with her, at a loss as to what to do. Amanda's breathing was labored, ragged, and out of rhythm. I asked to sit next to her and took her hand. In my heart I asked what I could do for her and heard her clearly say that her work was not done.

I leaned close to her. "You've completed your work here, Amanda, and done everything well," I said, squeezing her hand. "You can go now. It is safe for you to leave, and it is good.

You have done well in this life. You are dearly loved."

As I took a few deep breaths, it became clear that the other women and I should touch her and synchronize our breathing. The four of us gathered around, touching her hands, feet, and arms, sending love and gratitude to her. Within a couple of minutes, Amanda's breathing relaxed. The frantic beeping of the heart and blood pressure machines were becoming slower and steadier.

I whispered the Prayer of Protection in her ear: "The Light of God surrounds you, the Love of God enfolds you, and the Power of God protects you. The presence of God watches over you. Wherever you are, God is, and all is well." Then softly I said good-bye.

After thirty minutes, Amanda let go. For those of us flowing love to her, it was a great blessing to be present as she released her body.

Back at home, I went into meditation to connect with her to see how she was doing. She was ecstatic to be with the animals she had loved all her life and grateful to be free of her aging body. She was 74.

Amanda's passing reminded me how important it is to be present when someone is dying, and also that everyone is in charge of his or her own life and death. Offering love and permission to let go is all we need to do. Leaving our wishes for the person's survival out of the picture is imperative. It is always his or her choice. Our role is to support their choice, reassure them that they are loved, and release all judgment of what we think they should do. We cannot know what their path is.

Later, after they cross over, we grieve.

NOTES

15

Protecting the Heart

"Now, I have no choice but to see with your eyes.
So, I am not alone, so you are not alone."
Yannis Ritsos

When I was living in Texas, my son's father, Stan, retired from the Department of Probation and Paroles for the State of Tennessee and soon thereafter began to suffer heart arrhythmia. Doctors determined that he needed a pacemaker. Stan had been very fit, going to the YMCA five times a week, so this news was difficult for him to accept.

One morning during meditation I asked Stan if he would like to see the other side. As soon as I posed the question, he and I were standing in the Light Dome facing his family. His mom and dad were in front, with his grandparents behind them, as well as others I assumed were Stan's ancestors.

Stan's dad had suffered from PTSD and bouts of manic depression after serving in the Korean War, where he had picked up dead bodies off the battlefields. When Stan was eleven, his father took his own life with a shotgun, which placed a huge weight on the shoulders of his young family. Over the years, the ramifications of this act deeply affected Stan, his mother, and his siblings. There was so much pain that it did not feel safe for Stan to share his feelings with anyone.

On the walk, Stan's dad told him how remorseful and guilty he felt for having committed suicide. He was distraught because of the

85

pain he had caused his family, which had become unbearable for him. He felt torn up inside and convinced that no amount of love could soothe him. During the walk, he begged Stan for forgiveness and radiated love toward his son, asking that everything be healed. He knew it had been the hardest on Stan, since Stan looked so much like his father, and his mom had taken her anger out on him.

To my surprise, Stan turned to me to apologize and ask forgiveness for his behavior toward me during our marriage. Listening to his father, he realized what I had been asking for in our relationship – that is, for him to be more open with me and to be close to me. He would go to the local bar and have a good time, but at home he was guarded and would not let me see his feelings. When I first started seeking answers to our marital problems, I became aware that his commitment to weightlifting was another way for him to protect his heart by literally building a "hard body."

I was touched. I told him that we had not known how to do it differently and that I would always love him. We shared our gratitude for the role each had played in producing such a fine son. This exchange was an expression of our understanding that our paths had crossed for good and perfect reasons.

I cried for two days after I walked with Stan. I could see that my role in our marriage had been one of trying to fix him. It was more of the same pattern – my trying to fix everyone. From his perspective, I had not accepted him for who he was. I felt if I took care of the house and our son, I was doing my job, and he should do his. There was no partnership in our marriage. I taught school. He was a probation officer. After work, he often went to a bar and sometimes did not come home. Our time together was spent drinking, arguing, or sleeping – an unhealthy environment for raising a child. I had not realized how much distance there was between us until we separated.

As difficult as going through the divorce was for the three of us, I have never regretted the decision. The walk with Stan helped me to see the perfection in all that had taken place between us.

Several years later, Ray was with me when his father died from congenital heart failure while in hospice care. Immediately afterward, I sat with Stan again in meditation and saw him as a little boy with his baseball cap and glove on, hitting the ball into the glove, crying. He loved baseball, and nobody had supported him. No one had talked about his father's death or the fact that they needed to lean on one another. The family had swept the suicide under the rug, never calling it what it was. They had justified the suicide as an accident, and that was all Stan knew.

Stan's brother, Tom, was determined to get some answers for the family. After receiving some of his father's records from the Veteran's Administration, he discovered his dad had received new medication in the mail the morning of his death. Their dad had gone across the street to *his* father's home, closed himself into the back bedroom, taken off one shoe, and used a shotgun to end his life. Years later the family tried to get all of his medical records from the VA and were unsuccessful. They assumed, based on historical records, that the new medication might have been LSD. After examining what records he could get and the medical practices of the time, Tom came to the conclusion that the medication was causing his father to have hallucinations, which terrified him. Not knowing what was happening to him, he decided to end the pain. And to protect his family.

When I saw how heartbroken and alone little Stan was in that room, I understood much more about the man he had become. From the day of his father's death forward, he had done what he could to protect his heart by keeping distance from those he was closest to and loved the most. My life with Stan became clearer to me.

Since that time, I have had much more empathy and respect for the man I married. The walk brought the healing I needed. It allowed me to see beyond the illusion of our relationship to how we both did the best we could with the pain and trauma we brought into the marriage. His with the tragic loss of his father, and my life with the unresolved loss and grief brought about by the early death of my own father. As for Stan, I have never and will never stop loving him.

16

Walks: A Sacred Process

"Everybody can love in the place where they are.
We can all add our share of love
without leaving the room." Helen Nearning

Dear reader, I hope you sense the ease of the process described in these pages, one that you can use when you wish to feel helpful and more connected to those you love. The stories I've shared include taking someone on a walk to "the other side" when they are near death and feel uncertain and frightened about facing death. They also include connecting with those who are experiencing painful feelings and confusion for some other reason. Still, other stories involve connecting with those who have already passed on. The process can be helpful with family members and other loved ones, friends of friends, strangers, and, as you have seen, even animals.

The process is the same in all these circumstances. It involves setting an intention of being in a place of love and service, going into a space of deep peace within yourself, and inviting your loved one to a conversation and experience. A daily practice of meditation will deepen your experience and offer you more connections and insights. I encourage this, as it will bring you more peace in all your life experiences. Please be patient with yourself. Contact may happen immediately, or it may take an extended period of time of setting and holding the intention to connect.

Here is the process I follow as I prepare for and take a walk:

Come into a Place of Peace

Before you begin, come into a place of peace and silence through meditation and/or focusing on your breath. This may take just a few minutes, or it may take longer. Allow yourself the time you need to feel peaceful and relaxed.

Set an Intention

Then set an intention that is loving and compassionate. For example, when I walked with Big Dad, I asked to understand why he was so short with me when I was little. My intention when I walked with Mom was for her to find peace within her heart. Then decide on a question or two you would like to have answered. I suggest saying a prayer of protection along with your intention. I use "The Unity Prayer of Protection," written by James Dillet Freeman; however, you can create your own or use another prayer that gives you the feeling of protection from anything other than love during the process.

The Unity Prayer of Protection

The Light of God surrounds me. The Love of God enfolds me.

The power of God protects me.

The presence of God watches over me.

Wherever I am, God is, and All is Well.

Sacred Environment

It is important to create an environment that is sacred or supportive to you. Establish yourself in a place where you will not be interrupted by phones or other distractions. Light a candle or a stick of incense, or play meditative music if you like.

Location Does Not Matter

You do not have to be physically near the loved one. They can be in the same room with you or elsewhere. They can be "on the other side," having passed on. In the words of author Richard Bach, "There is no such place as far away."

Prepare Yourself

In the context of this process, connect to your Higher Self, the inner guidance that is a part of all of us, wiser and kinder than our ego usually is. Center yourself by taking several deep slow breaths and connecting to that inner guidance, which is based in love. As you breathe, picture your loved one. Continue this step as long as it takes for you to feel this connection. A simply breathing exercise that may help is to inhale to a count of four through the nose and exhale to a count of six through the mouth. Relax with each exhalation.

Ask Permission

Ask permission of the person's Higher Self or heart to connect with them on such an intimate level, stating that you intend to be of service in love. Affirm that only love is allowed. It is invasive to continue without permission. You will get a clear sense of permission, or a clear *no* that the person does not wish to make the trip. Once, when connecting with my brother, I received a definite *no*, and the session immediately ended. Don't try to force your will on the process. If you do, it is your ego-mind that has taken over.

It's Their Choice

Once you feel the person has given permission and you are connected, ask, "Would you like to take a walk to see what it is like on the other side? You are absolutely in charge." Or: "Is there some painful thing you would like help with or someone you'd like to connect with?" I make sure they understand it is always their choice and that I am only there as a guide, nothing more.

Questions You Might Ask

You can ask if there is someone on the other side that they would like to see or talk to. You can also just see what shows up. This is done in the etheric, not in person. My connection to the other side is my Aunt Otelia, whom I met on my first walk. You may have a specific person or being as a connection, or not. It is not essential that you have a guide or a connection such as Otelia. My experience with helping others has shown that the intention was the most important part of the process.

Your Experience Will Be Unique to You

After a few more breaths, my loved one and I are usually in a Dome of Light. The place may be different for you. Most important is to have no expectations or judgments about what should or does take place. Total loving allowance is what is required. Remember: only love is allowed, including love and compassion for yourself.

According to Suzanne Geisemann, Experiential Medium and teacher, this process took her three years to connect with her beloved stepdaughter once she made the commitment to do so.

When It's Finished

You will know when the conversation is complete. The person or animal will let you know they are ready to return or end the conversation, or that they choose to stay on the other side. It has only happened once with me that they chose not to return to the earth plane.

<u>Write Down What You Experienced</u>

After your walk, take time to write down what took place. You may be astonished by how much healing has happened for both you and the one who walked with you. Writing helps clarity and understanding to show up. It is always a sacred gift to experience walks with loved ones and others. I feel humbled and extremely blessed to share this loving experience with them.

The next few chapters include stories of other people using the process, more examples of how you may use this process.

NOTES

17

Alma Takes a Walk

"The best thing for being sad," replied Merlin,
"is to learn something." T. H. White

In the spring of 2013, I signed up for a creative writing course in San Antonio, Texas, hoping to make friends with the part of myself that would not let me write. The instructor asked us to introduce ourselves and say a word or two about why we were in the course.

"I am here to make peace with my saboteur," I told the group, "the part of me that shuts down my writing."

As we went around the room, a woman named Alma described how she always procrastinated when it came to writing. She looked across the room in my direction and stated she could relate to having a saboteur. The rest of the class laughed in agreement.

Alma came up to me at the break to introduce herself personally. We shared a few thoughts about ourselves and our respect for Caroline Myss, the author of *Sacred Contracts* which we both had read and studied. We discovered that we are both drawn to spiritual teachings and have explored a variety of belief systems, including Buddhism. As we shared our spiritual experiences, the friendship was sealed. After that first class we began to hang out at water aerobics and go for long walks on San Antonio's many walking trails while we shared about our lives.

Alma's mother was in a nursing home suffering from extreme pain caused by bone cancer. Alma was watching her mother deteriorate before her eyes, more so at each visit. Having gone through a similar experience with my mother a few years earlier, I felt much sympathy and compassion for what she was going through.

As our friendship deepened, I felt comfortable sharing the details of how I had walked with my uncles, my mom, and others to help them know what they might experience when they cross to the other side. I shared how these meditations helped me release worry and how I connected with each of them at a soul level through my heart to their higher selves. Alma was open to the process. She had been a meditator for years and understood what I was talking about.

That fall Alma and I attended a breathwork class together and began to practice that technique daily. As we practiced, Alma was able to connect more deeply with her mother during meditation.

<u>Alma's Experience</u>

My mom, Martha, was in a nursing home for eight years. As she approached the end of her life at 92 years old, I wanted to have a conversation regarding her wishes for her memorial service, but she was reluctant and uncomfortable speaking of death.

Barbara and I had many conversations about my worries and how they weighed heavily on my heart. I didn't know what to do. Barbara told me of a process she intuitively created in which she supports a loved one by taking them on walks to check out what they might encounter when they cross over the bridge to heaven while they are still in their body. Through meditation she takes a person on a mental walk to feel it out. I learned that I could do this with my mom, no matter where I was physically at the time. This helped alleviate my guilt for not spending more time at my mother's bedside and gave me some peace in our relationship.

While sitting with my mom in the nursing home when she was barely awake, I offered to take her on an imaginary visit to heaven.

We held hands as I described the exquisite beauty of heaven as I pictured it, the palpable peace, and the love that exists there. I could sense her relaxing while I imagined her taking it all in. During the walk, my mother became aware of the presence of my younger brother, who was hit and killed by a car at the age of eleven while riding his bicycle. He was vibrant and happy to see her. Mom glowed in the imagined experience. Her breath eased, and there was a slight smile on her face.

After this experience I felt more at peace and relaxed deeply into our relationship.

Invisible barriers lifted that neither of us had known existed. Then, two days later, she told me what she wanted for her memorial service and where it would take place, providing specific details. It was a beautiful and loving conversation about a topic that had previously been emotionally hard for both of us to discuss.

The process of taking Mom on her walk helped her release her fears and communicate her desires. It also lifted some of the dread and fear I had of losing her to the "other side." I will always be grateful for that experience.

Mom transitioned over four years ago, and I still use this compassionate process to have heart-to-heart visits with her. I often ask her questions about our life together. There was a great deal of turmoil in our household with five children and an alcoholic father who would rage and terrify us all. One of the questions that matters a great deal to me was, "Why did you stay with him?"

"What was I to do?" she said on one of the visits. "I have no marketable skills, and he did pay the bills. I learned to block out the rage and tried to ask Our Blessed Jesus to sustain me. I was so grateful you had church to cling to during those early years, and I know that's what got me through as well. Your brother and sisters and you were my priority. I learned I could get through most anything having each of you there for me. After losing Bobby, you are what sustained me."

It was after this visit that I understood the sacrifice my mother had made because she loved us. We continue to walk, and I hear her guidance whenever I ask for it. She is always with me.

18

A Mother Finds Peace

"The stuff in our lives doesn't change.
It is we who change in relation to it." Molly Vass

I recently received a phone call from Traci, a close friend who was concerned about her friend Donna. Two of Donna's sons had passed away only a year apart in similar bizarre circumstances, and Donna was overwhelmed with grief. Both of the sons had been alone when they passed, both under undetermined circumstances and not discovered for several days. During this time their bodies had decomposed considerably. Knowing of my walks with loved ones, Traci reached out for permission to give Donna my contact information, hoping the process might help her find peace.

I could hardly imagine how devastated a mother would be. Of course, I agreed, hopeful Donna would contact me. She called two days later.

"I am not a counselor, medium, or mystic," I said. "I do teach a process that can take someone on a sacred journey to connect with their loved ones on the other side or to assist them in going through a traumatic situation."

Donna told me about the circumstances of her son's deaths and the debilitating grief and anger she had been holding for over five years. Her oldest son, Ron, had struggled throughout his life with "not fitting in," as she put it. In his late 40's, he was very distraught and alone, having separated from the mother of his child. His body was found in their summer cabin alone, six days after he passed.

Even though the authorities expected he may have overdosed or made the decision to end his own life, an autopsy found no evidence of foul play or drugs in the body.

Donna's middle son, Matt, had also experienced bouts of depression and feelings of not belonging. He struggled with the meaning of life, his spiritual journey, and understanding his purpose. Also, in his late forties, he died in his apartment alone, with a Bible in his hands. He was not discovered for five days. Again, an autopsy showed no signs of foul play or substance abuse. Unfortunately, there were no answers for a distraught mother.

Donna also related that her third son, Norm, who is a gifted musician, had struggled with depression from an early age. His way of coping was to take recreational drugs, which led to a drug addiction. He was living in a rundown hotel, struggling to survive.

After our initial talk, I gave her the option of working with me to connect with her sons for answers to some of her questions. She said she would like to try the process. After all, she said, "What do I have to lose"? I asked if she meditated. Donna had meditated at one time but not in a long while. She also related that she had a fear of calling in negative forces since the deaths of her sons.

Following are the steps I gave her to begin the process:

1. Set a timer and meditate for at least five minutes a day. Although five minutes is a short time, for Donna it was a doable way to start. Increase your time as you are able, as more time will help you clear your mind. You can follow the natural flow of your breath, from your nostrils to your chest, feeling your abdomen expand, then follow the breath as it exits the body.

2. In your mind, set the intention to connect with one of your sons, with just one question you would like answered.

3. Continue the breathing until the timer ends the session. Increase the time each day as is comfortable. You can always go longer.

4. The most important part of the exercise is to write down the question. Then, after the meditation, write down the answer you receive.

The next time we spoke, Donna said she had followed the process and was delighted with her interactions with Ron. She realized that he had made the choice to leave, although he did not "hurry" his death in any way. He had chosen his death and did so naturally, without drugs or other suicidal means. He was finally at peace and had no regrets or shame about his life with her. He knew he had been a good son to her and assured her that he loves her and is always around.

Ron told her, "All you have to do is call my name and be still to feel my presence."

After her work with Ron, Donna decided to try to connect with Matt. She had a difficult time connecting with him in meditation, so I suggested she begin by writing him letters in order to express her grief, anger, and frustration of the past few years. After that, she was to write another letter, one in which she told him how much she loves him and all the joy he has brought to her life. Donna followed my advice and later shared that she had found peace with both of her sons after only four weeks.

One of the suggestions I made was to read *A Walk in the Physical* by Christian Sundberg.

She ordered it immediately, began reading and told me that it, too, had given her peace as she worked the process with her sons.

I am grateful for Traci sending Donna my way and for Donna's courage to think beyond what she thought might be possible.

NOTES

19

Much-Needed Apology

Grey and I have been friends for more than thirty years. We facilitated "Essential Peacemaking: Women and Men" workshops together and over the years have helped each other recover from traumatic life experiences such as divorce and heartbreak. Grey was trained as a Medical Qi Gong practitioner and also had computer skills that I had called on from time to time.

Grey grew up in the 1950s and 60s in West Nashville as the middle child of three. His father owned a construction business to provide for the family and was more absent than present. He sought out the company of women outside of his marriage, some mistresses and some one- night stands. He also hung out with his card-playing buddies instead of spending time with his family. When Grey was thirteen, his mother filed for divorce.

In 2009, forty-plus years after the divorce, Grey's father began to have health issues that affected his heart and stamina, and he asked Grey to move in with him. Although hesitant since their relationship had been stressful at its best, Grey agreed to move in with his father, as he had his own financial difficulties and a job he couldn't tolerate any longer.

Grey described his father as kind of a "godfather" in his not-so-plush neighborhood. He owned properties that he rented to alcoholics, drug abusers, and dealers. These were not Grey's kind of neighbors. It took Grey several months to convince them that his father was no longer in charge and that he, Grey, was changing the rules. After living with his father for a few years, Grey was able to establish some boundaries for himself and his father against the "users."

Eventually Grey remodeled the upstairs in his father's house and established an apartment for himself that provided more privacy than living on the main floor with his father.

As his father's health declined, Grey needed to do increasingly more to help with his care, which included grocery shopping, minor repairs around the home, and taking his father to doctors' appointments. Throughout this time, his father belittled Grey and argued about even the most minor expenses. It was not a peaceful situation, and Grey developed major health issues himself, unable to walk without pain.

In 2018, I visited Grey in his upstairs apartment to get some technical help with a new watch. While I was there, he shared the challenges he was having finding peace with his father, the demands his care required, and the toll it was taking on his own health. His father was declining rapidly and had almost died twice. As a Medical Qi Gong practitioner, Grey had been able to bring him back both times.

As we talked, I asked for permission to connect with his father. Grey agreed and set the intention to hear what his father had to share about their relationship. After setting the space for the walk together, we said a prayer, Grey lit a candle and asked to connect with his father.

We immediately found ourselves in the Dome of Light. Grey recognized his mother, who had died several years earlier, from photos of her younger years. His father was prominent in the center. Grey described the ancestors as white orbs behind them.

"I don't know how or what to do," Grey's father began. "I am afraid because I can't take care of myself, and I have to rely on you to do everything for me. I'm sorry I am such a burden and have been so hard on you. I know I don't deserve your commitment to me. I wasn't very good to you or the rest of our family. I was locked into my own selfishness and didn't know how to show love for any of you. It seemed the only thing I knew how to do was make money and that had to be enough." Grey listened intently to his father and conveyed the conversation to me.

Grey was a little shocked by this statement since he had never known his father to be vulnerable about what he was feeling. After a moment of silence, Grey told him, "I'm grateful to be able to care for you. I have also been afraid and angry at the distance between us, and I want more than anything to find peace in our relationship since we both know your life is coming to a close. I appreciate you meeting with me and sharing your fears. I do love you, although I don't care for the way you have treated me over the years. It is time to put all of that to rest."

I stood to the side as an observer and saw that the father looked young, about mid-forties with light brown hair. I heard exactly what Grey shared with me later.

Once again, his father spoke. "I'm so sorry for being so hard and cruel to you. You never deserved my anger. I am grateful you are my son and all that you have done for me. Thank you for meeting me this way. I promise to be more respectful through the coming months as I make my transition. Please know I am terrified of what's to come and need your positive assurance that all is well with us. That will make it easier."

In that instant we were back at Grey's kitchen table, both of us crying.

The walk helped Grey forgive his father and find some peace for them both. It seemed to have given him a better understanding of their relationship. We had several conversations over the next few months as his father continued to weaken and progress through the dying process. Since the walk, Grey had found it easier to understand his father and acknowledge the fear his father was experiencing as he had to depend on Grey more and more for his care.

After his father passed and Grey wrote his account of his relationship with his father, he told me that he had been able to get in touch with and release some of the anger and regret he had held regarding their relationship. Grey said that he had felt more peaceful after he worked the process and that living in his father's house had ceased to be as stressful as before.

20

Healing Ancestral Grief: My Story

*"How fascinating the idea of death can be.
Too bad, though, it just isn't true." Hafiz*

My great-grandmother passed away when I was eight years old and she was ninety-six. After her funeral, which was held at Big Dad's funeral home, the family gathered for the wake. While everyone milled around, I sat in the parlor that had also served as her bedroom. In the room were two chairs, a bed, and a coal-burning fireplace.

As I watched the fire, I saw her as clearly as if she were present. She was rocking in her small cherry rocker singing "Into the Garden of Prayer" with a clear, strong voice. As she sang, her long grey hair began to turn darker, and her wrinkles disappeared as she changed back into the woman of her youth. There was a beautiful smile on her face. She was radiant! I knew in that instant that I would be with her again. I missed her but found peace in knowing she would always be around.

While I was growing up, religious teachings were at the core of my family household. Our particular version of religion taught that God knows everything you do, and if you do not follow God's Law, you will live in eternal damnation, whatever that meant. Even as a child, I could not grasp that concept as truth. How could the all-knowing God, with such power and magnificence, give me one life to get it right before casting me into hell for all eternity? It did not compute, even to my young brain.

One morning during Sunday school, Mr. Petty called me out of class and gave me a "talking to" when I questioned the scripture of the day. I was twelve years old and in seventh grade. "Young lady, you realize that if you continue on your pathway of sin, questioning the Bible, you are guaranteed your place in eternal hell!"

I knew better than to argue with him, but I doubted his words. I also knew he was using scare tactics that were not going to work with me.

As I grew older, I did the best I could to adhere to what I was being taught. My family loved me, and I believed they would not lead me astray. I wrote the Lord's Prayer and the Twenty-third Psalm on butcher paper I bought at the store across the street and took great pains to make the posters perfect, then hung them on the door of my bedroom. I was dedicated to Jesus because He loved me, just as the song said. I decided to be baptized so I could be saved.

Over the next two years, as my body changed from a little girl to an adolescent, I was convinced I had sinned. I found out that I liked boys and had my first kiss. Heaven forbid! I needed to be saved again, so I went before the church and got baptized a second time. I had bought into the idea that "God will get you for that." I never really knew what *that* was, but I was convinced I had done it and wasn't taking any chances.

By the time I was eighteen and in college, I gave up trying to make sense of teachings that seemed unattainable. Once, while sitting in the balcony at church listening to what I called bullshit under my breath – I remember it had something to do with the "lust of the body" – I quietly stood up, left the church, and walked down the street to my boyfriend's house.

I muddled through the next twenty-five years with little thought about the God of my youth. I graduated college, got a teaching job, married, and had a child. I put aside my Christian upbringing and went through life taking care of what was in front of me without any thought of tomorrow, trying to control the circumstances around me as much as I could. I wasn't happy and knew something was missing, but I didn't know what. My husband and I drank excessively, and the emotional distance between us caused many arguments. His absences grew longer as he preferred a bar stool to spending time with me and our son. I realize now that my nagging and ultimatums didn't make it very comfortable for him to stay home with me.

My marriage fell apart after twelve years, and in my grief over the loss of my marriage, I began spiritual studies with a determination to live my life differently.

"What do you see yourself doing if you get a divorce?" a counselor asked me. I answered without hesitation. "I want to find out why I have done this to me."

I knew no one had made me live like this – drinking, blaming my misery on everyone else, and complaining about everything and everybody. My mantra was, "If everyone would do what I wanted them to do, everything would be right in my world." Why had I made such poor choices?

While looking for answers, I explored past life regression where I had an experience that changed how I saw myself in relation to my husband and my son. A counselor guided me to relax, breathe, and still my mind. After several minutes, I observed myself outside a log cabin by a fire over which hung a large iron pot, stirring what appeared to be clothes. I was a heavy set woman in a long black baggy dress with a kerchief around my head. A young boy of seven years old stood near me begging. I recognized him as Stan, my husband in this life.

"Mom, please let me go to the river. I'll be careful. I just want to see how high it got. I won't go near it, I promise," he pleaded.

This was very odd because the boy had never asked for anything. He was a quiet child who stayed to himself and wanted very little to do with his sisters. The river was the only place that seemed to bring him joy. How could I refuse him, even when my better judgment told me to say no?

After I gave my permission and he took off in the direction of the river, a strange feeling came over me. I quickly emptied the pot of clothes and went after him, calling him back as I went. I reached the river just in time to see him leap into the rushing water. He did not stay visible for long and was gone in an instant.

I froze on the spot, screaming and yelling for help. His father came running from the nearby field. I recognized him as my son, Ray, in this life. He could not console me. He took me back to our cabin, gathered our daughters, and left to go get a neighbor for help and took our daughters with him. After he left, I flew into a rage, throwing furniture, dishes, anything I could grab, to express my despair. When my energy was spent, I collapsed on the floor near the fire. I did not realize I had thrown a quilt over the fire, which began to smolder and fill the cabin with smoke. When Ray returned with the neighbor, I too was dead.

What I experienced may or may not have been another life I have lived, but the experience brought me peace and an understanding of why I had been so determined to do whatever I could to make Stan happy. It seemed that I had been born in this lifetime with a job to "fix" everyone. The effects of this pattern are still something I recognize today in all my relationships.

Awareness of this pattern has made it much easier to let it go. As I processed what I had relived, it was clear to me why Stan and I had come together. I realized that I had been determined to make his life better, to make him happy on my terms, regardless of the cost to my own happiness and a complete disregard for his own desires. I never took into account that he was responsible for his own happiness. In my attempt to get him to live "my way," I had made him more miserable and our lives a torment for both of us.

Over the next several years I became determined to learn more about life after death. The idea of one life per soul had never made sense to me. I read many books about past life experiences. The appendix includes a list of the books that helped me the most. My visits with Big Mama as she shared her stories about Otelia, and the realization that I had been Otelia, became clearer and more real with every book I read. As my grandfather, my father, friends of the family, and other loved ones passed on, I found myself connecting with them in dreams and through journaling. I began to meditate more and focused on connecting with specific souls.

Studying has brought me to the understanding that we all have a soul contract in each lifetime. This contract is designed for our soul to experience certain opportunities that will enhance the soul's progression into deeper love for the self and others. In *The Little Soul and the Sun*, author Neal Donald Walsh includes a beautiful description of how we choose our soul's life lesson. Other souls in our "soul group" agree to play certain roles for us, Walsh explains, in order for us to learn specific lessons and achieve our goals of a particular lifetime.

I understand now how the members of my family tree have played roles that enabled me to release the guilt I carried because of my choice, as Otelia, to leave the planet at the age of four. I have always felt responsible for others' pain, wishing I could do something to fix it, as I have shared throughout this book. I have not taken into account that everyone has their own contract when they come into form. Today I believe that everyone who is related to or comes into contact with a soul has agreed to play a part in the soul's growth, progressing toward releasing the perception that they are separated from Source, from God. I like to think they all auditioned for the part.

This puts grief in an entirely different category for me. The grief I've experienced around the loss of a loved one has a different meaning when I understand that everything happens for a reason, toward the evolution of all the souls involved. Sadness, pain, and sorrow are very real feelings, and I do not mean to diminish them in any way. But we have free will to process each loss in our own way. Understanding that our perceived losses can teach us about the connections that exist through eternity makes all the difference in how we relate to the death of those we love.

When a soul incarnates and experiences various possibilities for healing, it is their choice to heal or not. Because my lifetime as Otelia was so short, the possibilities for love and healing that were created by that early death were enormous. Now, in this lifetime I can accept responsibility for the grief, anger, and sense of loss I left behind and assist my family in healing. Did they ask me to play that role for them? I believe they did. Did I accept the role of peacemaker and healer in this lifetime? I believe that I did. It is because of that role that the visions came to me, I initiated the walks, and I wrote this book.

Life offers infinite possibilities. What I believe and how I live with those beliefs is my greatest responsibility.

Recommended Reading

---*A Course in Miracles.* Los Angeles, CA: Foundation for Inner Peace, 1976.

Bach, Richard. *There's No Such Place as Far Away.* London: Delta Publishing, 1998. Callanan, Maggie and Patricia Kelley. *Final Gifts.* New York: Simon & Schuster, 1992. Giesemann, Suzanne. *In the Silence.* U.S.A. One Mind Books, 2014.

Gibran, Kahlil. *The Prophet.* New York: Alfred A. Knopf, 1923. Greaves, Helen. *Testimony of Light.* New York: Penguin Group, 2009. Hanh, Thich Nhat. *No Death, No Fear.* New York: Penguin Group, 2003.

Jampolosky, Gerald G., M.D. *Love is Letting Go of Fear.* Berkley, CA: Celestial Arts, 1979. Kahn, Matt. *Everything Is Here to Help You.* Carlsbad, CA: Hay House, 2018.

Kahn, Matt. *Whatever Arises; Love That.* Boulder, CO: Sounds True, 2016.

Kubler-Ross, Elizabeth. *On Death and Dying.* New York: The Macmillan Co., 1969. Lipton, Bruce, PhD. *The Biology of Belief.* Santa Rosa, CA: Elite Books, 2005.

Ladinsky, Daniel. *A Year with Hafiz.* New York: Penguin Group, 2010. Moorjani, Anita. *Dying to Be Me.* Carlsbad, CA: Hay House, 2012.

Nepo, Mark. *The Book of Awakening.* San Francisco: Conard Press, 2000. Oliver, Mary. *New and Selected Poems.* Beacon Press. Boston, 1992.

Parry, Danaan. *Warriors of the Heart.* Cooperstown, NY: Sunstone Publications, 1991.

Peters, William J. *At Heaven's Door.* New York, NY: Simon and Schuster, 2022. Selig, Paul et al. *I Am the Word.* New York: Penguin Group, 2010.

Ray, Sondra. *Loving Relationships.* Berkley, CA: Celestial Arts, 1980.

Renard, Gary R. *The Disappearance of the Universe.* Berkley, CA: Fearless Books, 2003.

Singer, Michael A. *The Untethered Soul.* Oakland, CA: New Hampshire and Noetic Books, co- publishers, 2007.

Sundberg, Christian. *A Walk in the Physical.* Erie, PA: Christian Sundberg, 2021.

Tolle, Eckhart. *The Power of Now.* Novato, CA: New World Library, 1999.

Tucker, Jim B. *Life Before Life.* New York, NY: St. Martin's Press, 2013.

Walsch, Neale Donald. *The Little Soul and the Sun.* San Francisco, CA: Hampton Roads Publishing, 1998.

Williamson, Marianne. *A Return to Love.* _New York: Harper Collins Publishers, 1992.

Recommended Websites

 https//www.awalkinthephysical.com. Interviews and a download of the book is available; also on YouTube.

https//www.TTouch.com. "A complete explanation of the Tellington Touch Method" that Amanda used with animals; also, on YouTube.

https//www.suzannegiesemann.com. Information on the programs and teachings of Suzanne Giesemann; also on You Tube.

https://www.zachbushmd.com. Information on the programs and teachings of Dr. Zach Bush; also, on YouTube.

https://www.sharedcrossing.com. Information on the research programs conducted by William Peters and associates.

https://www.jimbtucker.com. Information on the author and links to recent research and books.

About the Author

Barbara Jill Eatherly grew up in middle Tennessee with her parents and three brothers. After completing university, she embarked on a forty-plus year career in education as a teacher and administrator. She also studied esoteric teachings and healing modalities such as Transference Healing and Mayan Astrology. An avid reader and researcher of mystical teachings, she studied near death and shared crossing experiences and many New Thought teachings.

Today Barbara lives near Nashville, Tennessee, where she conducts workshops on The Walk Process and offers private sessions for those who want to connect deeper with their loved ones.

Contact Barbara at info@thewalkprocess.com